CONTENTS

ARMOR
FROM ANCIENT TO MODERN TIMES

PETR
KLUČINA
PAVOL
PEVNÝ

BARNES
&NOBLE
BOOKS
NEW YORK

Text by Petr Klučina
Illustrations by Pavol Pevný
Cover and graphic design by Václav Rytina
Translation by Jan Šach and Hana Veselá

Original edition copyright © 1992 Slovart Publishing Ltd., Bratislava
English translation © 1997 Slovart Publishing Ltd., Bratislava
This edition published by Barnes & Noble, Inc., by arrangement with Slovart
Publishing Ltd.
ISBN 0-7607-0475-9
Printed in Slovakia by Neografia, a. s., Martin
97 98 99 00 01 M 9 8 7 6 5 4 3 2 1

PREFACE

Humans have made and used weapons since the beginning of time. Weapons made hunting possible. It also allowed people to defend themselves from becoming the prey of animals. The need to protect one's tribe from the attack of another inspired the development of protective armor. What does *protective armor* mean exactly? It is the name for all the components of a warrior's equipment which provide passive protection against an enemy's attack.

Protective armor consists of various features. The *protective outfit* is the most important component, because it covers more or less the entire trunk of the warrior. A *helmet* and a *shield* are other key features of protective armor. The shield proved essential in warding off enemies' weapons. The earliest armor components were very primitive and made of plain materials easily found in nature. Fur, leather, and sometimes bark, wood, and bones (i.e., skulls of large animals could be used

Gold helmet *from Pre-Columbian America. It originates from Colombia and is probably a product of the Indian tribe Quimbaya.*

for helmets) were the most common materials for early armor making. Fur, for example, could dull a blow, while armor made from animal bones was effective at deflecting arrows.

The real evolution of armor or its so-called golden age, started by 3000 B.C. with improvements in the technology of metal processing. Metal began to predominate as an essential material for armor making (although the former materials such as leather, fur, cloth, and wood were never completely discarded). Throughout history, armor was prohibitively expensive. For this reason, the privileged classes of any period were the owners of the most sophisticated armor. Armor became a status symbol and as such was richly decorated. Early armor was influenced by a number of factors: the availability of materials, the level of metal-processing technology, and the types of fighting done and weapons used at the time.

Chimalli (shield) *ascribed to the Aztec monarch Ahuapoth. The picture is created as a mosaic of colored feathers accented by a border sewn with gold thread.*

Local and contemporary trends and traditions dictated to a great extent the form a suit of armor would take. Armor was as much a fashion statement as it was protection. Because wars and battles have inspired artists to paint and poets to write, we are surprisingly well informed from literary and artistic works about the evolution of protective armor. Wall paintings, frescoes, portraits, illuminations, and the like depict warriors in full suits of armor. The art of sculpture has given us many priceless treasures using the motif of armor. Perhaps most important, archaeological excavations have unearthed many pieces of the original armor itself. Indeed, metal armor has been preserved primarily due to its material, which wasn't meant to be easily destroyed. Many of these fascinating armor artifacts are on display at major museums. Together with historical documents, they provide us with a historical outline of the development of armor and its cultural context.

Wig helmet *of Prince Meskalamdug from grave no. 755 of the royal burial site in Sumerian Ur. It is made of electrum and dates from the middle of the third century B.C. It was probably a symbol of royal power.*

FROM HEPHAESTUS' WORKSHOP

During the fourth and fifth millenniums B.C., the first states were formed in fertile areas around big rivers — in Africa at the Nile, and in Asia Minor at the Euphrates and Tigris. The protection of these city-states was ensured by their armies. While the armor and the organization of these armies varied, their importance to the safety of all city-states was crucial. Armor needed to be improved to protect the soldiers from increasingly sophisticated bronze weapons. For example, when attacked, Sumerian foot soldiers hid themselves behind big, oblong wooden shields and lined up side by side, presenting the enemy with what looked like a living wooden rampart bristling with lance tips. The heads of these soldiers were also protected, either by pointed leather (probably padded)

caps or copper helmets. Only a small number of soldiers belonging to the aristocracy or royal guard could afford such enormously expensive armor. By 2500 B.C., the craft of metalwork was so developed that it could produce armor of artistic value. The beautiful wig *Meskalamdug's helmet* attests to this sophistication. Created in the middle of the third millennium B.C., the wig was discovered at the royal burial site in the Sumerian town Ur.

While shields and helmets were the Sumerian soldier's most important means of protection, heavy coats or wraps of sheep's fleece were worn into battle. One of the reasons for the comparative lack of body armor was the warm weather — heavy clothes were inappropriate for marching along the riverbanks of the Nile in the summer. Therefore, soldiers of the Old and

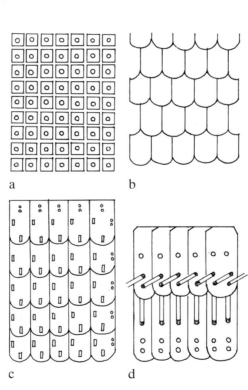

a   b

c   d

Reconstruction of the armor of a Sumerian dignitary. *His body is protected by a thick cloak and a kilt of sheep fleece. He wears on his head a copper wig helmet.*

The basic types of the ancient protective outfit:
a) *plate – made of small metal plates riveted onto the garment*
b) *scaled – having scales attached to the garment*
c) *scaly – having scales fastened with a strap, such as one illustrated in* **(d)**

Mycenaean warrior in full armor. *He has a helmet on his head, and his body is covered by a leather kilt and leather greaves. A large, hourglass shield helps ward off enemies' weapons in battle.*

Bronze helmet, circa ninth to seventh century *B.C. The high crest and richly engraved ornamentation marks this helmet as from the Villanovan period in Italy. This helmet is now housed in the museum in Saint-Germain-en-Laye in France.*

Middle Kingdoms (2686 – 1991 B.C.) wore linen kilts (loincloths). In order to protect their sparsely clothed bodies, Egyptians carried shields. It was not until the New Kingdom, or the second half of the second millennium B.C., that the garments became more varied. The New Kingdom brought with it protective outfits called *linen armor.* Linen armor consisted of several layers of strong linen strengthened by quilting bound with leather straps. Sometimes leather, cotton padding, or even thin metal plates were interwoven between the layers of linen. Egyptians tended to protect their heads with massive wigs or quilted caps rather than helmets. Conversely, the foreign mercenaries of the pharaohs wore helmets and the pharaohs themselves donned *helmet crowns.*

Scaly mail, a type of all-metal armor, arrived in Egypt from the Middle East during the period of the New Kingdom. It was shaped like a short-

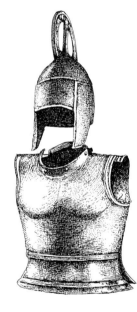

Greek bell mail with helmet, *the typical armor of the heavily armed warrior in the eighth century B.C.*

sleeved tunic extending to just above the knee, and its surface was covered by flake-shaped metal plates. Scaly mail was one of two popular protective outfits in the ancient Near East. The other popular tunic was *plate mail* made from tiny square or oblong metal plates attached to a leather or cloth kilt.

While building their empire between the eleventh and seventh centuries B.C., the Assyrians were pioneers in the use of armor. Some Assyrian mail consisted of a short vest reaching to the waist, while others covered the body to mid-thigh. The armor of the heavy infantry was even more ingenious, covering the warrior from head to toe in a tunic to which metal plates were attached. However, the high point, literally and figuratively, of the Assyrian's armor was the helmet. Made completely of metal or of leather strengthened at the lower edge with metal hoops, these helmets were conical or semicircular and decorated with variously shaped metal grips to hold horse hair tufts.

Assyrian shields varied not only in shape and

Triple-disk breastplate of a cuirass. *This cuirass was used by a member of the Samnite tribe.*

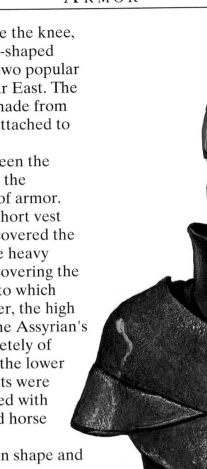

A full suit of armor, circa mid-fifteenth century B.C.
This unusually heavy armor probably belonged to a military dignitary who fought from a chariot, making the unwieldy weight of the armor less important. The armor (including greaves, remains of a shield, and a boar helmet) was found in chamber grave no. 12 on the hill Midea at the Greek colony Dendra.

size, but also in their use of materials. The most common was a large, circular leather shield that had a metal bulge in the center surrounded by smaller wooden bulges. Other types included a round wicker shield and a huge, oblong wooden shield mounted with metal, which in battle could hide both the archer and the shield bearer. A staggering amount of armor was used by the warriors in the Far East and Asia Minor;

the great variety of armor made the armies vibrantly colorful. Armor of the Persian Empire influenced weaponry and armor across Europe, and particularly in Greece, which through frequent wars and waves of migration, was in the process of establishing its own empire. This influence brought on a peak in armor and weaponry, as Homer attests in the *Iliad*:

*This type of **bronze breastplate made by Greek craftsmen** and decorated with the head of Medusa was often used by Scythians.*

Corinthian-style helmets *were heavy, but offered complete protection to the soldier's head and face. Tradition ascribes this bronze helmet to Miltiades, the commander of the Greeks in the battle of Marathon. It is housed in the museum in Olympia.*

First he shaped the shield so great and strong, adorning it all over and binding it round with a gleaming circuit in three layers; and the baldric was made of silver. He made the shield in five thicknesses, and with many a wonder did his cunning hand enrich it.... Then when he had fashioned the shield so great and strong, he made a breastplate also that shone brighter than fire. He made a helmet, close fitting to the brow, and richly worked, with a golden plume overhanging it; and he made greaves also of beaten tin.

In the *Iliad* Homer describes the armor made for the hero Achilles by the divine blacksmith Hephaestus. It is clear that it was a real masterpiece. These verses introduce the full suit of armor used by some of the best-known warriors of ancient times — the members of the Greek heavy infantry, the *hoplites*. The whole suit of armor of the hoplites was called *panoply* and included a helmet to protect the head, mail and a shield to protect the body, and metal *greaves* to protect the legs from the instep to the knee.

In the Mycenaean period a caste of savage, fearless warriors fought either on foot or in

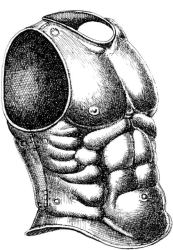

Reconstruction of the appearance of typical muscle mail. *This type of mail was used not only by Greek warriors, but also by Etruscans and Romans.*

Thracian helmets *were the favorite type of helmet in Greece. This bronze helmet from the fourth century* B.C. *is decorated with volutes and boasts a neck guard and movable cheek plates. It was found in Gavarnie and is now housed in the Brail Museum in Romania.*

chariots. The chariot, a sort of ancient tank, had long been a dreaded war vehicle. From inside the chariot, warriors could launch spears or shoot arrows into the enemy lines. In the Mycenaean period, the crew of a chariot included a charioteer and an armed warrior. The warrior wore heavy mail consisting of several bronze plates, which protected him down to his knees, as well as metal greaves and a helmet. Archaeologists found such armor during excavations in Dendra. But not every Mycenaean soldier wore plate mail. Many wore

clothing in the form of a short-sleeved, midthigh-length made of two layers of cloth. Quilted between the layers were bronze plates — twenty to twenty-two larger plates and ten to twelve smaller ones. To protect themselves, other soldiers had to make do with shields. Large, oblong shields, made of leather stretched over a wooden frame, covered the soldier's entire body. The smaller hourglass-shaped shield typically had an octagonal wooden frame and was made to cover the whole soldier. Boasting a massive central rib reinforced with strips of

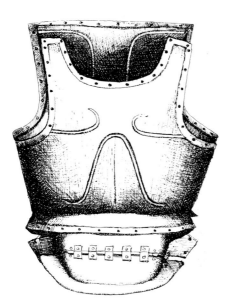

The breastplate of a Greek cuirass.
The Greek cuirass followed the muscles of the male body. The soldier's groin was protected by a short plate attached to the front plate of the cuirass.

*This richly decorated **helmet** probably belonged to a Dacian dignitary. It was almost certainly made by a Greek craftsman, but its shape and decoration indicate the influence of Scythian and Iranian art and many local features. It was found accidentally in 1928 in Romania on the site of the Dacian-Gothian settlement from the La Tène period.*

Typical **bronze greave** *used by Greek hoplites (fifth century B.C.).*

Celtic shield from the first century A.D. *found in the Thames at Battersea. It is made of a bronze plate and decorated with wrought ornaments with enamel fillings. The inner side was probably lined with wood. The shield is 77.5 cm (30.2 in) high and apparently was not used for battle, but for religious ceremonies.*

Bronze Celtic helmet *decorated with horns, found in the Thames and dating from the first century* A.D. *It is made of thin plate, and its construction is very delicate. Therefore, it is probably a ceremonial helmet, not for use in battle.*

Bronze helmet of the Bosporan style, *originating from the territory settled by the Scythians.*

wicker, the shield was covered with sturdy leather. Small, round shields were also popular and are depicted in figures and wall paintings (i.e., in Cadmée). The helmets of the Mycenaean soldiers were either leather caps with small metal plates attached at the top, or bronze helmets that covered the cheeks and had a socket on top, in which a horsetail tuft was planted. An example of the latter was discovered at Tiryns.

Perhaps the best-known Mycenaean helmet is the *boar helmet.* The boar helmet was a leather helmet strengthened with sinews and felt, and decorated with several neat rows of boar fangs. Several works of art from the period allow us to see what the boar helmet looked like, and remnants of the fangs themselves have been excavated.

Bronze Celtic helmet, *probably from Italy. It has movable, pendant cheeks and a short neck guard. It dates from the middle La Tène period (the third to second century B.C.). It ranks among the helmets known from excavations on the territory of the Senones tribe. These helmets were the basis for the standardized helmets of the Roman legionaries used until the beginning of the first century A.D.*

Reconstruction of the appearance of a Celtic warrior. *Celtic warriors fought partially or completely naked and protected themselves with a large wooden shield. This warrior wears a typical Celtic helmet.*

When the sun had set on the Mycenaean civilization, Greece took its place as one of the greatest cultures in history. First comprising only the territory now known as Greece, the ancient Greek state expanded to include the coastal areas of Asia Minor, the Black Sea, northern Africa, Sicily, southern Italy, and France.

The strength of the Greek army lay in the fact that every male citizen was armed and prepared to fight to defend the state. A citizen's armor reflected his financial status which in turn was expressed in his position in the army.

The hoplites were the most prestigious branch of the army. They were armored foot soldiers, who in a neat line would attack the enemy's forces at close range. In so doing, they gained a reputation for inspiring terror. In the eighth century B.C., the hoplites tended to wear uniform armor. This standard armor was well represented in the armor discovered in Argos. Bronze bell-shaped cuirasses, or mail, consisted of breast- and back plates worn on the body, while a heavy helmet covered the face. Finally, bronze greaves and a round, bulged shield

Helmets inspired other headgear, for example, this **gold Scythian helmet crown.**

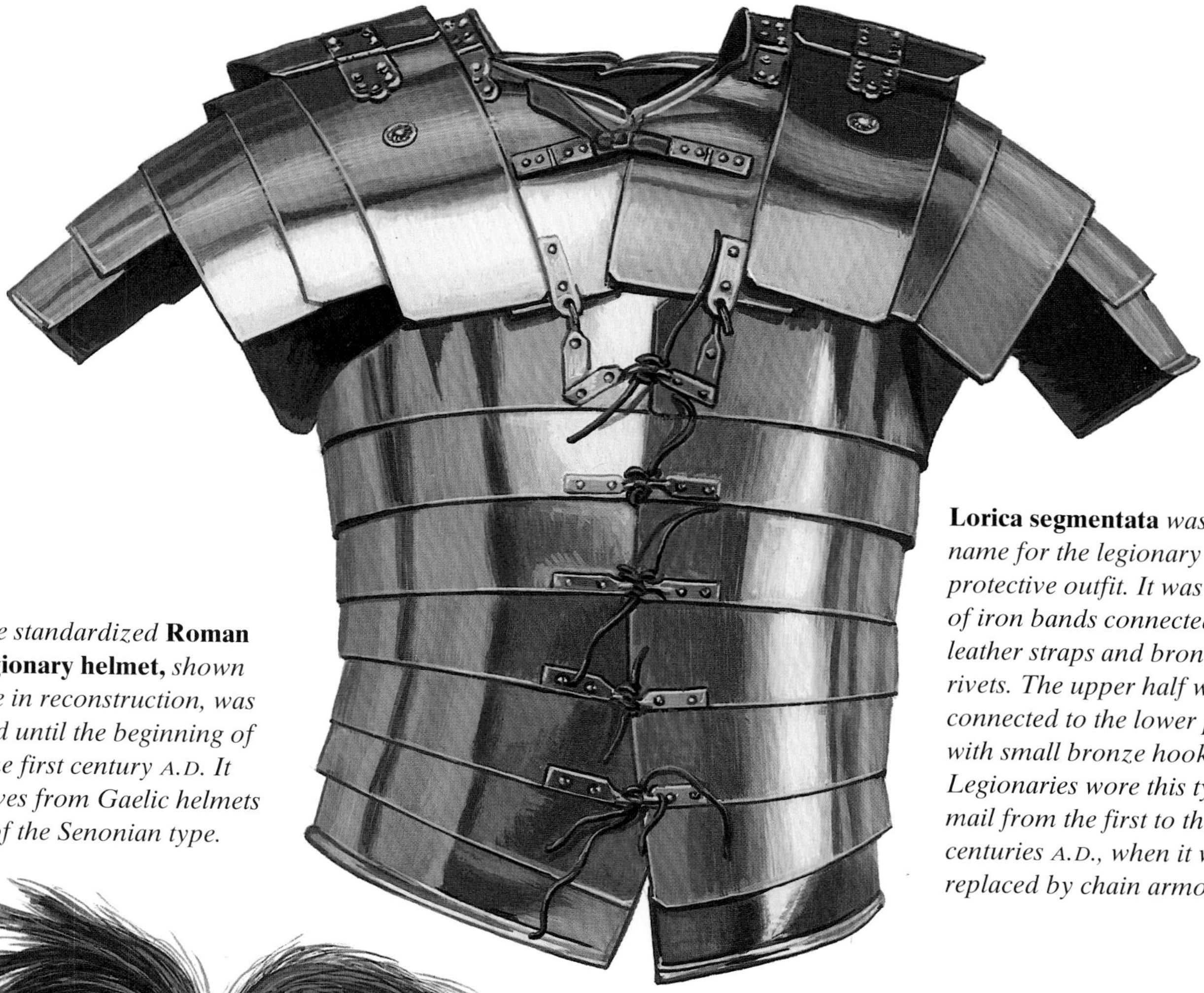

*The standardized **Roman legionary helmet,** shown here in reconstruction, was used until the beginning of the first century A.D. It derives from Gaelic helmets of the Senonian type.*

Lorica segmentata *was the name for the legionary protective outfit. It was made of iron bands connected with leather straps and bronze rivets. The upper half was connected to the lower part with small bronze hooks. Legionaries wore this type of mail from the first to the third centuries A.D., when it was replaced by chain armor.*

*The Imperial Gaelic style **iron galea,** shown here, had a wide neck guard and anatomically contoured cheeks. This type of helmet also derived from Gaelic patterns used by legionaries from the first century A.D.*

mounted with bronze completed the armor of the prestigious hoplites.

The hoplites' armor changed little between the eighth and sixth centuries B.C. There are many reasons why armor was not developed to protect parts of the body left vulnerable to attack. Covering the arms and forearms, thighs, or feet with metal plates greatly limited the soldier's ability to move; moreover, the plates were uncomfortable. Bronze bell-shaped mail, however, was so successful that its use spread to other parts of Europe, including as far as France, Switzerland, Etruria, and central Europe.

Particularly wealthy members of the heavy infantry boasted their own armories within their homes. The poet Alkaios described one of these armories in a poem, paying tribute to helmets with fluttering horsetail tufts, metal greaves, linen mail, and bulged shields. Gradually, the armor of the common Greek warrior grew in sophistication. The most important piece was a large, round, slightly bulged shield, which

*This extravagant **Roman cavalry helmet** was discovered in a grave from the first century A.D. during excavations of a Roman villa in the village of Tchatalka in Bulgaria. The skull of the helmet is made of iron, while the facial part is made of silvered bronze. Together with the helmet, a full suit of armor for a mounted soldier, including cuirass, leg coverings, shield, spurs, two swords, fifty arrow tips, and six lance tips, were found.*

Hellenistic soldier in a full suit of armor. *Equipped with a **sarissa,** or long lance, and a typical helmet and chain mail derived from Celtic patterns, this soldier was clearly one of the mass spearmen of the phalanx.*

protected the warrior from neck to midthigh. The shield's exterior was bronze, its center was wooden, and its interior was lined with leather. A metal grip, often ornamented, hung from the inside of the shield, which was meant to fit the warrior's forearm comfortably. On the interior of the shield, a cord was usually strung from one side to the other. This cord allowed a marching soldier to carry his shield on his shoulders. The

shield, or *aspis*, was painted with a symbol known as an *episema*. Sometimes this was an embossed decoration made of metal. A popular episema was the head of the Gorgon.

While the shield was the most important part of a Greek soldier's armor, it was supplemented with mail that protected the body. *Linen mail*, consisted of back and front pieces and big *pauldrons*, or shoulder guards, tied at the back.

In Rome, fighting games on horseback, a prototype of medieval tournaments, were connected to the cult of the dead and were quite popular. To prevent injuries, the *armor protected not only the fighter but also his horse. An example of horse armor is the* **bronze forehead plate from the first half of the third century** A.D., *shown here.*

The front ends of the pauldrons were tied up to the ring on the breastplate of armor. The armor was made of layers of strong linen strengthened with inserted metal plates or with plates of bronze scales attached to the top layer. The armor extended no further than the waist. It owed its success to its light weight which allowed for movement, while providing good protection to the wearer. Later, to address the need for protection below the waist, *pteryges,* or wings, were created. These oblong metal flaps were attached between the layers of linen and hung around the whole mail to midthigh.

The second type of armor originated from the ancient ideal of beauty invoked and worshipped by the Greeks. The aptly named *muscle mail,* a bronze cuirass with front and back plates, followed the muscular lines of a man's body. Helmets soon followed the same trend. Up until the end of the sixth century B.C., Corinthian helmets, which protected and outlined the head of the warrior (except his eyes), had dominated. They were gradually replaced by similar but lighter Chalcidian, Illyrian, or Ionian helmets — all of which boasted movable cheek plates. Light helmets of the *pilos* type, such as the Thracian and Boeotian helmets, were popular during the Greek-Persian wars, and they were also common, in a slightly altered form, during the Hellenistic period.

From the fifth century B.C., bronze greaves worn on the leg were decorated. Made of a single piece of metal, the greave had a slit in the back, which the hoplites opened to put the greave on. When closed, the greave clenched the

Legionary in full suit of armor. *Here a legionary is depicted wearing an iron helmet and holding a scutum — a large shield mounted with metal.*

Gladiator in full suit of armor. *This reconstruction shows a soldier bearing a sword and large shield and wearing a gladiator helmet with a grating visor, arm covers made of metal strips, and a metal greave on the leg that in a fight is moved forward closer to the enemy. For gladiatorial fighting, trained fighters were equipped with many weapons and covered with extensive protective armor.*

leg all around. As a full suit of armor weighed 30–35 kg (66–77 lb), one or several servants would carry it for the hoplite during regroupments.

Specialized craftsmen were responsible for producing increasingly sophisticated armor. In Greece, craftsmen of armor formed a *collegium,* or guild. Master craftsmen worked for the Scythian aristocracy. As the work of the Greek craftsmen made its way to the Greek colonies, the Greek style of armor became widespread and influenced the armor of "barbarian" nations, such as Thrace and Dacia. Greek armor, in turn, reflected outside influences. For example, mercenaries of barbarian areas brought to

Greece certain types of light shields (pelts, etc.). Nevertheless, in spite of some adaptations and peculiarities of style, the basic armor of a foot soldier in the Hellenistic period changed little. The same basic armor served the Greek foot soldier whether he was fighting in Asia Minor, the Far East, Egypt, Thrace, Italy, Carthage, Sicily, Sardinia, or on the Pyrenean peninsula. As an army, a comparable rival hardly existed — that is until the legions of Roman soldiers formed.

For centuries, the Romans fought for their independence with the many enemies that occupied them — be they Etruscans, Samnites, Heruli, Aequi, Volsci, or Gauls. As their

*The skull of this **mask helmet from the first century** A.D. was made of iron, while the facial mask and laurel wreath were made of silver. This mask was found in a necropolis of a Roman village called Trimonticum at what is present-day Plovdiv, Bulgaria.*

territory grew, the Romans inevitably came into conflict with Greek city-states in Italy, Sicily, and Carthage. With the defeat of Carthage, Rome took its place as a great power on its way to world rule. Their growing empire would not have been possible without Rome's outstanding army, the main arm of which was the heavy infantry.

Not unlike other civilizations, the Romans learned much about armor from their opponents.

In the eighth century B.C., Romulus is said to have founded Rome during the time the Villanovan culture was flourishing in some areas of Italy. Archaeological digs have unearthed bronze helmets from this period that have a high, spiked crest made of two pieces riveted together. The body of the warrior was mainly protected by an oblong plate measuring 15×22 cm (5.9×8.6 in) and fastened with leather straps. The warrior wore a similar plate on his back. A poncho-shaped armor plate

*The **Sarmatian cataphract** was a heavily armed soldier on horseback, who wore scaly armor and a helmet. The Sarmatian and Parthian heavy cavalry were serious rivals of their Roman counterparts.*

provided shelter of a higher quality. Shields were round, 50–100 cm ($19\frac{1}{2}$–39 in) in diameter, and made of bronze. They were held by a handle placed in the middle of the shield. There may also have been shields woven out of willow wicker and covered with leather. This was the basic armor used in Italy at the time of Rome's foundation.

Not all Roman Republican legionaries were equal. Roman legionaries were classed according to financial status. Much the same as the Greek hoplites, the best-armored soldiers were the

*Roman **heavy cavalryman** completely covered with metal, inspired by Parthian models. Scaly mail also covered the rider's horse. The rider's seated position was stabilized by a saddle the Romans adopted from mounted Celtic soldiers.*

wealthiest. The armor of the rich Roman even mirrored that of the Greek hoplite. The light-armored foot soldier wore a rather simple type of helmet, and his chest and back were protected by smaller oblong or round bronze plates fastened with straps. For all soldiers, the most important accessory was the *scutum*, a large wooden shield. The origin and shape of the scutum is unclear. One theory argues that it was first an oval shield with a handle in the middle, as Livy described. Another theory is supported by

*This **gladiator helmet,** shown here in reconstruction, was worn at victory parades.*

Dionysius' and Diodoros' mention of an oblong shield. It appears that the bronze figures of warriors found in Vetulonia may give us the best portrait of the scutum — an oblong shield with rounded corners and a central metal bulge.

The Celtic or Gaelic contribution to the evolution of armor cannot be underestimated. It was only after battling with Gaelic tribes that the Romans saw the need for the standardization of legionary armor. From the Greeks, the Romans had adopted the helmet with its movable cheek protectors and a small protector for the nape of the neck. This Greek helmet had been the standard of legionaries until the first century A.D. Then the Greek *hauberk,* or padded tunic, was replaced by a Gaelic-style chain hauberk, which imitated the style of Greek linen armor. This protection was supplemented by the *legionary scutum* – a big, flexible, oblong wooden shield covered with leather and reinforced with metal mounting.

Gaelic helmets, in all their variety, set the pattern for legionary helmets. The Celts originated all of the following features regularly found in the equipment of legionaries from the first century A.D.: iron helmets with small forehead shades, ear protectors mounted with copper, large cheek protectors, and a broad protector for the nape of the neck. However, the greatest contribution of the Gaels was the invention of *chain armor* – armor made of a network of closely connected chains. The genius of chain armor was its ability to protect while not impeding movement. The Romans were not the only ones to copy Gaelic chain armor; the Hellenistic states also seized upon the idea. The Gaelic tribes that penetrated through the Bosporus to Asia Minor brought chain armor to that region, too, where it eventually became the most popular type of protection for a soldier. If the Celts had a weakness, it was their shields, which were thin and made of wood. As Caesar wrote, it was possible to get through several of the shields with a single, heavy spear.

During their victorious campaign for world rule, the Roman legions swept the Hellenistic infantry off the battlefields, along with the Asian armies of mounted soldiers and foot infantry.

They defeated the Gaelic tribes and withstood the German onslaught for a long time.

There was a wide variety of armor used by the Roman troops. Commanders wore metal or leather muscle mail in the Hellenistic pattern, foot soldiers wore chain mail or leather coats, and mounted soldiers donned scaled hauberks. The average member of the legion wore armor that proved its worth in many battlefields of the time. It consisted of a heavy helmet with a big protector for the nape of the neck, banded mail (*lorica segmentata*), and a heavy, oblong shield — the scutum.

In the Orient, the legionaries met with one surprise: the heavily armored mounted soldiers of the Sarmatians and Parthians. Scaled armor covered the entire body of the mounted soldier, and his horse was protected by a *shabrack* covered by metal plates. Using bows and long, heavy lances, the mounted soldiers brought death to many Roman legionaries. Soon the Romans created a similar cavalry in their army. The craft perfection of this armor is incomparable. Roman aristocracy spared no expense in decorating the armor made for themselves and their horses. Nor was the purpose of armor confined to battle. It was also used in ritual combat connected with the cult of the dead. Many pieces and, in some cases, full suits of armor have been found by archaeologists and are proudly housed in the world's most important museums.

The fall of the Roman Empire took its toll on the development and maintenance of armor. Foreign mercenaries left the crumbling state, taking their fighting capabilities and their armor with them. Craftsmanship and metal processing in the weakening empire deteriorated as barbarian tribes penetrated Rome's frontiers and devastated once flourishing towns and villages. Barbarian tribes were most devastating to the Western Roman Empire, which had enjoyed strong traditions in military art and protective armor. The Eastern Roman Empire, however, persisted for many centuries — it was known as Byzantium. In Byzantium and in the Orient, the tradition of armor craftsmanship survived.

This richly decorated **helmet of the latter Roman type** *was found in Pannonia.*

THE GOLDEN AGE OF ARMS AND ARMOR

The fall of the Western Roman Empire meant much more than changes on the map of Europe; it also entailed the decline of the technology of metal processing. Soldiers arose whose effectiveness was not compromised by their more primitive armor. Nevertheless, vestiges of the armor of the ancient world and the influence of Asian armor persevered for a long time.

Soldiers of the expanding Frankish empire were mostly protected by wooden oblong shields, strengthened with a central metal bulge. The body was covered by a garment of thick leather strengthened by rectangular metal plates attached close together. For centuries the *ribbed helmet* was very popular, the origin of which is probably in Sassanian Persia. It was quite simple to make, and provided good protection for the soldier's head. Helmets of similar construction were used until the beginning of the fourteenth century. It is, however, important to note that it was a very expensive piece of armor, which could be owned only by members of the upper class.

As military practice increased, armies were formed, with the heavy cavalry as its most important faction. In the time of Charlemagne, soldiers used armor that consisted of a helmet (either ribbed or with a broad edge), a short tunic covered with metal scales, and an oblong shield. Strong leather straps were wrapped around the calves to protect the legs.

Ribbed helmet from the sixth century A.D., *found in Chalon-sur-Saône in France. The helmet is made of six ribs joined on the top of the helmet's skull by a small copper plate, which has a socket for a tuft. On the inside, iron reinforcements are fastened between the ribs. The ribs are decorated with rich embossing; the band around the lower edge of the helmet is made of dark red copper. It weighs about 950 g (33.3 oz).*

During this period in Europe, chain armor became more ingenious than ever before. Scandinavian raiders, who had troubled Europe since the ninth century, perfected chain armor. They were able to do so because of the easy availability of high-quality metal in their territory, a long smithing tradition, and their trade connections with the Orient. An Irish chronicler wrote with astonishment of how the Scandinavian raiders outdid their opponents in wearing so much shiny and reliable armor. Northern European armor has been discovered in archaeological digs in Scandinavia (Vendel, Sweden) and England (Sutton Hoo). The quality of the craftsmanship is astonishing.

The helmets of the leaders were perfect works of art — they contained semicircular iron skulls, or coverings for the top of the head, and were richly decorated with bronze bands ornamented with geometric and figural imprints. While some had cheek plates, others had fixed chain hoods. The nose was protected by a *nasal*, which was usually a piece of metal attached to a helmet.

Leather helmets were also worn. However, even the helmets were surpassed in sophistication by the chain tunics of various lengths. The shield was wooden, round, painted, and reinforced with a central bulge. On the sides of a famous excavated Osebarian burial ship, yellow and black shields were hung alternately as decoration.

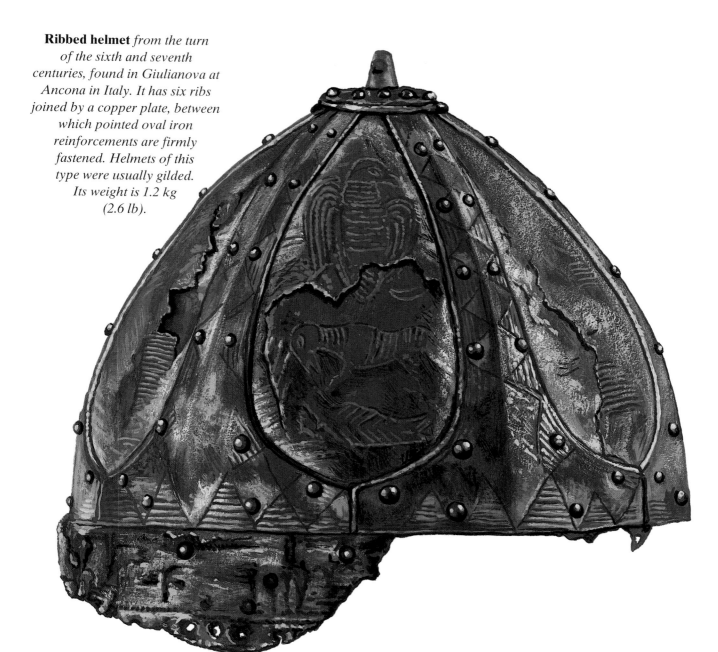

Ribbed helmet *from the turn of the sixth and seventh centuries, found in Giulianova at Ancona in Italy. It has six ribs joined by a copper plate, between which pointed oval iron reinforcements are firmly fastened. Helmets of this type were usually gilded. Its weight is 1.2 kg (2.6 lb).*

Vikings wore armor made of metal plates attached to a cloth or leather garment, but they also wore cheaper protective outfits made of traditional nonmetal materials. When leather was hardened by boiling, it provided the fighter with relatively solid protection. Over the course of the seventh to twelfth centuries, Europe saw a variety of simpler and more sophisticated armor. Sophisticated armor never came cheaply. The Ripuarian law of the seventh century states that plate armor was of the same value as two stallions, a helmet was worth one stallion, and a shield was worth one bull. The entire armor and weaponry of a heavily mounted Caroline soldier, including his horse, had the same value as a herd of forty-five cows.

By the eleventh century, heavy cavalry dominated European battlefields. A cavalryman was a carefully and individually trained professional and a master of his weapons, be they the heavy double-edged sword, the lance, ax, or mace. He had been trained to fight and ride since youth. Fighting was an ordinary part of life for a knight. In battle, the king himself took great risks, as knightly honor required him to lead the army into battle and set an example for his subjects by fighting bravely. The armor of the knight needed to give effective protection while allowing him to concentrate on offensive activity.

The beautiful Bayeux tapestry, which records the history of the conquest of England by

Iron-ribbed helmet from the sixth century, *found in Slovakia at Dolné Semerovce. It has four ribs, between which iron pads are fastened. It is decorated with gold and silver.*

William, Duke of Normandy, tells us much about the fighting styles of the time. In the tapestry, one can identify the heavy cavalry from the hooded protective outfits that reach to the knees and have slits in the front and back. Materials for protective outfits varied. Some outfits were made of strong cloth to which oblong or square metal plates were attached close together. Other outfits, similar in construction, were made with scaly armor.

The most perfect protective armor was *mail* — the long, chain tunic. A good example of chain mail is preserved in the treasury of Saint Vitus in Prague. It belonged to Saint Wenceslas and dates back to the tenth century. The protective outfit was supplemented with leather boots which had straps that the fighter pulled around his calves up to his knees. These straps were sometimes strengthened with rivets or metal plates. The so-called *Norman helmet* was conical and had a nasal set on the hood. The smith made the helmet out of one piece of plate or several, riveted from within to a frame formed by iron ribs, in much the same way a ribbed helmet was made. An extremely large, kite-shaped riding shield strengthened with mounting completed the armor. Hung on a strap over the knight's left shoulder, the shield protected the knight from shoulder to instep.

On the one hand, armor was a functional matter; on the other hand, it was also a symbol of the social position, prestige, and wealth of the

Gilded ribbed helmet from the sixth century, *found in Dolné Semerovce in Slovakia.*

wearer, and was therefore often decorated. Helmets and plate armor were silvered or gilded; the combination of plates and scales made of various materials (e.g., iron or bronze) could create an interesting effect on a plate or scaly outfit. This effect could also be created by the intentional coloring of the surface (by silvering or gilding). Helmets could also be gilded or silvered, or the skull could be covered by dyed leather. In written sources, "painted" shields

also are often mentioned. Shields covered by parchment or leather were dyed (red was usually a popular color), or there were various symbols painted on them.

The great variety of armor persisted into the twelfth century. The coat of armor gradually became shorter as the protective outfit was supplemented by hose, which was either covered by plates or scales, or made of chain netting. Conical helmets remained popular up to the

The armor of a Viking leader. *A helmet with a slit for the eyes, a chain hood, and a leather jupon strengthened with iron bands (discovered in grave no. 8 in Valsgarda in Uppland) complete the protective armor of this warrior.*

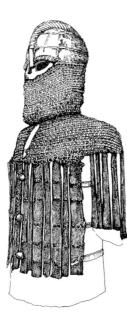

Pre-Viking helmet from the seventh century A.D. *It is made of iron and decorated with bronze plate imprinted with ornamentation. The warrior's face is protected by a curved piece of metal around the eyes and a massive nasal. It originates from grave no. 1 in Vendel, Sweden.*

second half of the twelfth century, when they were replaced by helmets with semicircular skulls. They were forged out of one or two pieces of plate metal, and strengthened by a banded brim around the circumference and one iron band running from the forehead across the helmet spike to the nape of the neck. These strengthening bands also were usually gilded or silvered, and formed decorative parts of the helmet. At that time, a smaller shield had not yet been made, but the bending of the shield's upper edge into a kite shape disappeared. In the twelfth century, *caparisons* appeared for the first time. Quilted or chained, caparisons protected the knight's horse against wounds.

The thirteenth century became the golden age of arms and armor. Knights found use for their equipment in a context other than war, though

*A heavy **truncated helm** from the second half of the fourteenth century.*

often no less life-threatening: the medieval tournament. As the medieval tournament gained in popularity and prestige, armor took on an international perspective. Hitherto, there was little difference in the appearance of a knight from France and a cavalryman from Bohemia or Austria. In the thirteenth century, however, armor became the basis of the knight's protection; specialized craftsmen were able to forge distinctive helmets, hose, and shields. The knight's chain tunic reached to the middle of his thighs or knees and was supplemented by a hood and gauntlets made of several thousand rings joined together. Chain hose added extra reinforcement. Weighing only 10 kg (22 lb), the tunic was flexible and didn't limit motion. Many knights wore a chain hood over a special padded cap, but the best protection was provided by a heavy *great helm,* which covered the knight's entire head and face and had a narrow slit for the eyes. A rounded triangular shield gave protection from shoulder to waist. Over his chain armor, the knight put on a long, sleeveless tunic, or *surcoat,* that either bore his coat of arms or his heraldic colors. His coat of arms was also imprinted or painted on his shield.

A set of armor made by the famous armorers of Milan. *The armor includes a plate cuirass, helmet, leg coverings, and gauntlets. The cuirass weighs 2.65 kg (5.8 lb) and consists of several overlapping plates decorated around the edges. On the right side there is a lance rest. The helmet's (Hundskugel) chain veil attaches to the top of the cuirass. The movable visor is decorated with a bronze brim and inscribed with a quotation from the Bible. The complete suit of armor originates from the 1390s and is housed in the armory in the château Churburg.*

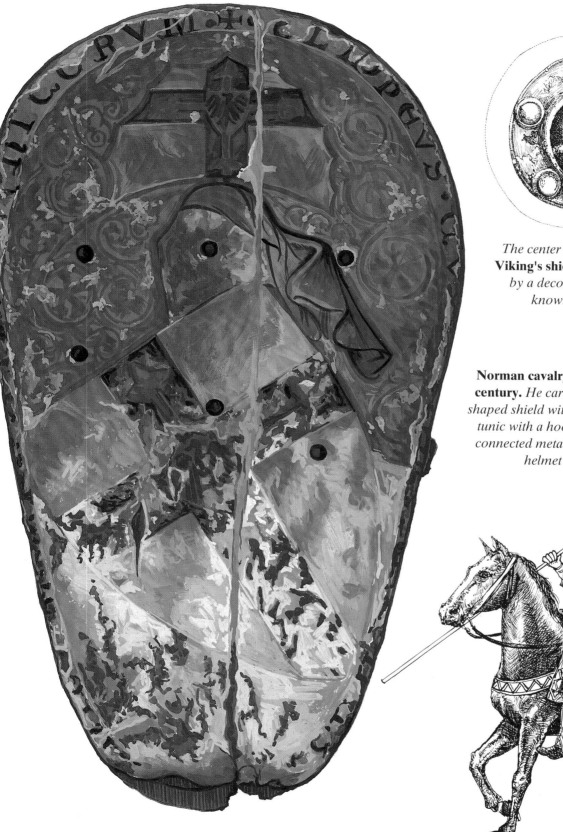

The center of a round wooden **Viking's shield** was strengthened by a decorated metal bulge, known as an **umbo.**

Norman cavalryman of the eleventh century. *He carries a typical almond-shaped shield with a metal bulge, a long tunic with a hood covered by closely connected metal plates, and a conical helmet with a nasal.*

Pavis (riding shield), *which belonged to Charles of Trier, the grand master of the Teutonic Knights (c. 1300). The pavis is made of wood and decorated with the grand master's coat of arms.*

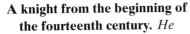

A knight from the beginning of the fourteenth century. *He wears a visorless helmet with a chain veil onto which could be fastened a heavy truncated great helm for use in battle. His body is protected by chain mail and hose, with plates reinforcing the protection of forearms and knees. A cloth surcoat with a coat of arms is worn over the outfit. There are (typical especially of the French region) rectangular plates called* **ailettes** *covering the knight's shoulders. A triangular shield completes his equipment.*

Pavis shield *for civilian militia from the second half of the fifteenth century, with the Prague coat of arms.*

The sophistication of metal processing enabled new and improved types of armor to be made. For example, the sensitive parts of the soldier's body, especially his joints, were covered with plate pieces for the first time in the thirteenth century. This protection was first in the form of knee plates. It wasn't long before this new armor was gilded and engraved. The plates that followed were oblong or rounded and covered the shoulder joint.

By the end of the thirteenth century, swords were used more and more as thrusting weapons, since chain armor didn't provide effective enough protection against thrusts. An attempt was made to eliminate this disadvantage by strengthening chain armor with iron bands or oblong plates riveted to the inside of the fighter's garment to give twice as much body protection. Some of these garments, made of reinforced cloth or leather were shaped like a poncho and pulled over the head.

The fourteenth century was a century of searching. Although chain armor was still very popular and made in many variations, it was supplemented by an increasing number of accessories. It was either a plate vest strengthened as just described, or a *brigandine* or *jack,* a padded or quilted vest or coat. Besides protecting the knees, plates soon protected elbows as well, and leather, reinforced with steel or strengthened with rivets, also covered forearms, arms, thighs, and shins. As time passed, chain armor was replaced by oblong metal plates. Iron plates in vests were becoming bigger. In the second half of the fourteenth century,

An example of **Gothic armor.** *The beautiful, well-designed armor was made by Augsburg armorer Lorenz Helmschmied for Archduke Sigismund of the Tyrol around 1480. The pieces of armor are joined by rivets and leather straps. The typical protection for the head is a salade with a movable visor supplemented by a steel chin piece (missing here). The peculiarity of this suit is the thigh protection. Instead of a thigh-length tasset, there is metal hose with overlapped plates.*

Armet, *the first type of closed helmet for a complete suit of plate armor. It has a movable visor, a chin piece fastened by a leather strap, and the remains of a chain veil or camail for covering the neck and shoulders. This armet was made in the workshop of the famous Milanese armorers Gabriel and Francesco Merate around 1495.*

large plates covered the entire breast and back. By the second half of the fourteenth century, complete suits of plate armor had been perfected.

Many specialized crafts were involved in the making of armor. In fourteenth-century Europe, craftsmen in regions famous for excellent armor quite often supplied distant countries with their products. The workshops of armorers in northern Italy, especially in Milan, were very famous. The art of making armor was also developing in Germany. Armorers became some of the richest and most popular craftsmen. Helmet makers also were in demand, as the variety of helmets grew rapidly. The flat-topped great helms were replaced by heavier, more pointed helmets, which were attached to the shoulders by means of chains or leather straps. Although they protected the head perfectly, great helms limited vision and were heavy and uncomfortable to wear. Therefore, knights often put them aside and were content with other types of helmets. Henceforth, great helms were used exclusively at tournaments.

The *basinet* was an open-faced helmet worn by the soldier going to battle. It was made from a single piece of plate and was designed more ergonomically than any helmet that preceded it. The basinet had a *camail,* or chain veil, attached to the lower edge of the helmet, reaching to the wearer's shoulders, breast, and back, thereby doubling his protection. This helmet usually didn't have a nasal. It was sometimes fixed to the chain veil at the mouth level. It was possible to lace the top of the veil to eyelets in the front of the helmet. This helmet covered the whole face except for the ears and a part of the face, where the chain was attached. The basinet could be fitted with a plate visor or a movable grating, which allowed the face to be well protected without the heavy great helm.

In the second half of the fourteenth century, the visor was usually made in the picturesque shape of an exaggeratedly long dog's nose. The *dog's-face* (Hundskugel) was the most popular knightly helmet at the turn of the fourteenth and fifteenth centuries. The *great basinet* was a variation of the dog's-face, in which the

Richly decorated barbut from the end of the fifteenth century *made in Milan. At the present time, it is in the collection of the state-owned château Konopiště in the Czech Republic.*

Reconstruction of a knight *wearing a full suit of armor from the beginning of the fifteenth century, based on an engraving on the tombstone of Rudolf of Baden. The knight wears complete plate armor supplemented by a helmet with a dog's-face visor and a smaller shield.*

Iron salade with fixed visor. *It is decorated with a brass scroll along the lower edge, and was made in central Europe in the 1470s.*

latter's chain veil was replaced with a metal *gorget,* a massive plate that fit over the shoulders and covered the throat.

Because plate armor did not have refined surfaces, most knights wore over their armor a *jupon,* a close-fitting tunic made of expensive fabric. Knightly shields took on a variety of shapes over the course of the fourteenth century, but the most notable invention was a slit in the shield through which the knight could thrust his lance during battle. This slit not only protected the knight, but actually helped him aim his lance at his opponent more accurately. Soon, a rest for the lance was attached to the breastplate of the armor. The fifteenth century saw the greatest boom in the art of armor, when full plate armor with chain accessories became standard.

By the end of the thirteenth century, Milan had earned its reputation as the most important center for armor. Competition for this title came mostly from Germany, most notably from the town of Nuremberg. By the fifteenth century, armor guilds had grown in the German towns of Augsburg and Landshut. Innovations in armor craftsmanship came from the Italians and Germans, while craftsmen in Paris, Tours, Lyon, London, and Burgos (Spain) tended to imitate them.

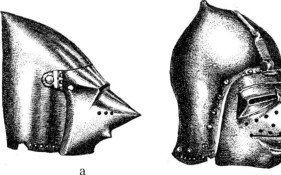

a

b

Two of the most common knightly helmets *of the end of the fourteenth and the beginning of the fifteenth centuries:*
a) *Northern Italian helmet from 1400*
b) *German helmet from circa 1400–1420*

Frequent, long-lasting wars and tournaments kept the demand for weaponry and armor high. Amid this heavy demand, armor craftsmen and, indeed, the craft itself, flourished. For example, the extent of the demand was such that when Emperor Charles IV feared that Bohemia would be invaded in the 1360s, he ordered that all members of the urban militia in the Czech kingdom be supplied with armor. This meant that even in a small town of a thousand inhabitants, approximately one hundred suits of armor were to be made for the local militia. This figure is even more impressive when one considers that only the poor needed their armor subsidized. The wealthier members of the population ordered their armor themselves. Moreover, the armor made for the Czech urban militia was imported from Germany. This international "armor trading," if you will, was quite common. Indeed, English noblemen and French knights regularly ordered their armor from Italian craftsmen.

Some Italian craftsmen even worked abroad. A record exists of an Italian master in the fifteenth century making armor in the French town of Tours, and there is evidence of other Italian craftsmen working at around the same time in Lyon and Bordeaux. The Emperor Maximilian I hired fifty Italian armorers in Arbois, Burgundy, to make him fifty suits of armor at the end of the fifteenth century.

Italy boasted an extraordinarily large number of armorers. In the fifteenth century, there were in Milan alone two hundred craftsmen whose specialization was armory. The most renowned craftsmen came from the Missaglia family. In fifteenth-century Germany, armor crafts flourished in Augsburg, Landshut, and Tyrolean Innsbruck, and continued to flourish in Nuremberg. These craftsmen made use of advances in not only the processing of metals such as iron but also the processing of metal additives. These advances made it easier for armorers to polish the armor so well that it shone, making unnecessary the traditional cloth tunic that covered the armor for decorative purposes. By the 1440s in Germany, the centuries of experimentation and expertise

Torso of **jousting armor** *made of polished steel in upper Italy around 1500.*

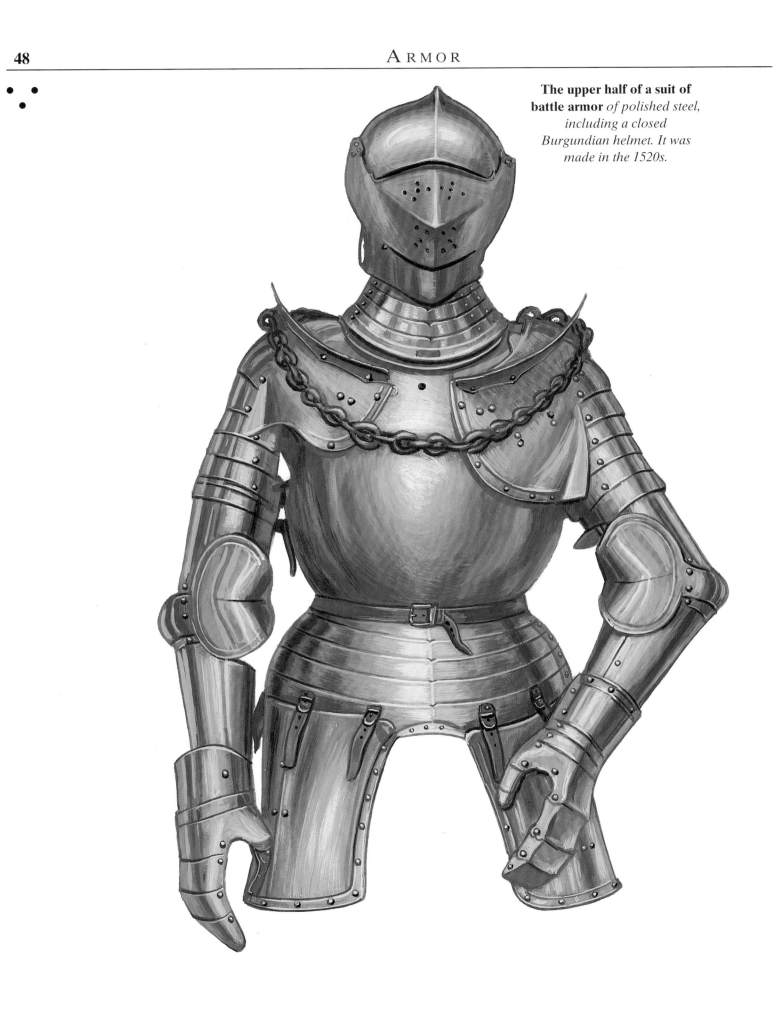

The upper half of a suit of battle armor *of polished steel, including a closed Burgundian helmet. It was made in the 1520s.*

● ● ●
●

German **jousting armor**
(in German, Stechen)
made around 1500 in
Nuremberg by the
armorer Konrad Poler.

Armor of King Louis II as a child, *made by Nuremberg armorers in the early sixteenth century. The armor is silvered and gilded, and it includes a Burgundian helmet consisting of six pieces. The armor is embossed with fretting in imitation of a fabric pattern.*

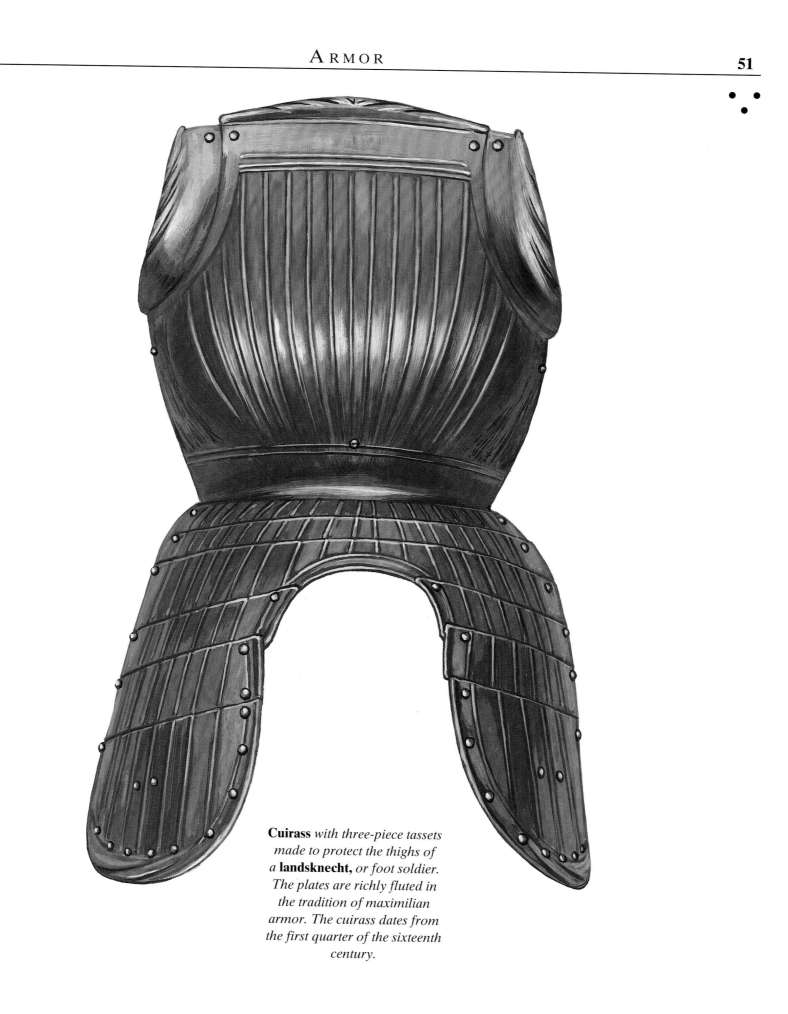

Cuirass *with three-piece tassets made to protect the thighs of a* **landsknecht,** *or foot soldier. The plates are richly fluted in the tradition of maximilian armor. The cuirass dates from the first quarter of the sixteenth century.*

resulted in a remarkably refined style of armor, called *Gothic armor.* Gothic armor dominated the second half of the fifteenth century. Sometimes, Gothic armor included plate covering the thighs, as well as a plate *beard,* or drinking visor, which covered the mouth area of the helmet. Additionally, a helmet called the *German salade* was typically worn with Gothic armor. Nearly all the pieces, be they cuffs of *gauntlets,* long *tassets* or thigh guards, *rerebraces* or upper arm pieces, plate boots, and so on, were spiked. German craftsmen made armor for horses, too. Equestrian armor consisted of anatomically contoured metal plates, the design of which displayed the same trademark clarity and elegance as the soldier's armor. Gothic armor reached its heyday in the 1490s.

As noted earlier, the fourteenth century witnessed a shift in the function of armor. While armor's original use was for the battlefield, the tournament, a prestigious contest, required a different type of armor. It would be wrong to assume that the tournament required any less protective armor than that used on the battlefield. Tournaments of the fifteenth century were a very dangerous form of entertainment in which participants were wounded or killed on a regular basis.

As the tournament was a key social event for proving one's worthiness as a knight, many knights were willing to take life-threatening risks

Equestrian armor,
made by German armorers in the year 1450.

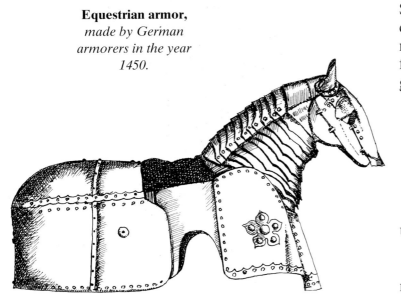

in the *jousting tournament.* Armor that ensured maximum protection was called for. Therefore, thick plates of metal were used in jousting armor. At the same time, jousting armor needed to allow for a wide range of movement. Certain suits of armor were designed for the joust, while others were intended for the *foot combats.* Tournament armor revealed local peculiarities and unlike the more primitive battlefield armor of several centuries prior, it would have been easy to distinguish between an Italian knight and a German knight.

By the end of the fifteenth century, the first Renaissance armor, called the *maximilian armor,* came into existence. Its form was influenced by several factors, most centrally the taste and fashion of the times and the need to perfect the armor's protective ability while not thickening the metal plate of which it was made. Armorers achieved these goals by covering the surface of the armor in thick fluting. This exquisite armor was so difficult and costly to make that it saw active duty for no longer than thirty years. After 1530, it simply disappeared from the battlefield. Craftsmen developed a similar type of armor with a surface that imitated the look of precious stones by grinding pyramid-like shapes on the surface of the armor. In fact, maximilian armor became the last battlefield armor worn by knights.

In the fourteenth century, a new infantry appeared on the battlefield, replacing knights. Swiss, Hussite, and English archers were able to crush knights in battle partly due to their use of missile weapons. Increasingly, armies were formed using mercenaries who needed to wear good, but cheap and functional, armor. Mercenaries wore simpler types of helmets, too, such as the iron, broad-brimmed *kettle hats,* salades, and *barbuts,* which were simple bucket helms with a single face slit. Their bodies were protected by either a *brigandine,* a plate vest, or by several plates covering the breast and back. The mercenary's legs often went unprotected.

The rise of the mercenary infantry put a definite end to knightly military service, but it by no means marked the end of the history of armor.

THE END (AND GLORY) OF THE ARMOR CRAFT

By the end of the sixteenth century, heavy cavalry had seen its heyday. In spite of manifold attempts on the part of sovereigns to modernize and reorganize cavalry, their effectiveness on the battlefield had been outlived. Firearms and progressive strategies of mercenary infantry made knightly units in battle obsolete. The battle at Novara in 1513 is a classic example. In this battle, the Swiss infantry effortlessly crushed the French knights. Because their armor could deflect arrows, but not gunfire, knights became defenseless targets in this more modern warfare. Thus, armor passed from serving a function to being purely a status symbol. Armor was now being made for noblemen to wear at ceremonial

Trabant, or three-quarter armor from the second half of the sixteenth century.

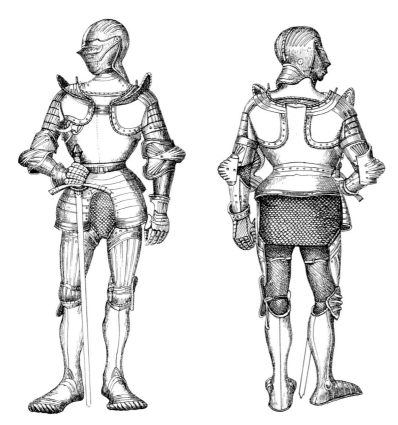

Full plate armor from the beginning of the sixteenth century, *when plate armor was fully developed in terms of its technical execution and the number of its features. It consisted of a helmet, a gorget, a cuirass (front and back plates), a metal belt, a belt kilt (skirt), and thigh tassets (Schwänzel) attached to the skirt. Protection for the arms included (from top to bottom) a pauldron, a metal sleeve, an elbow piece, or couter, called a "mouse" in eastern Europe, a forearm covering, and gauntlets. The legs were covered with thigh plates, knee pads, calf plates, and metal boots.*

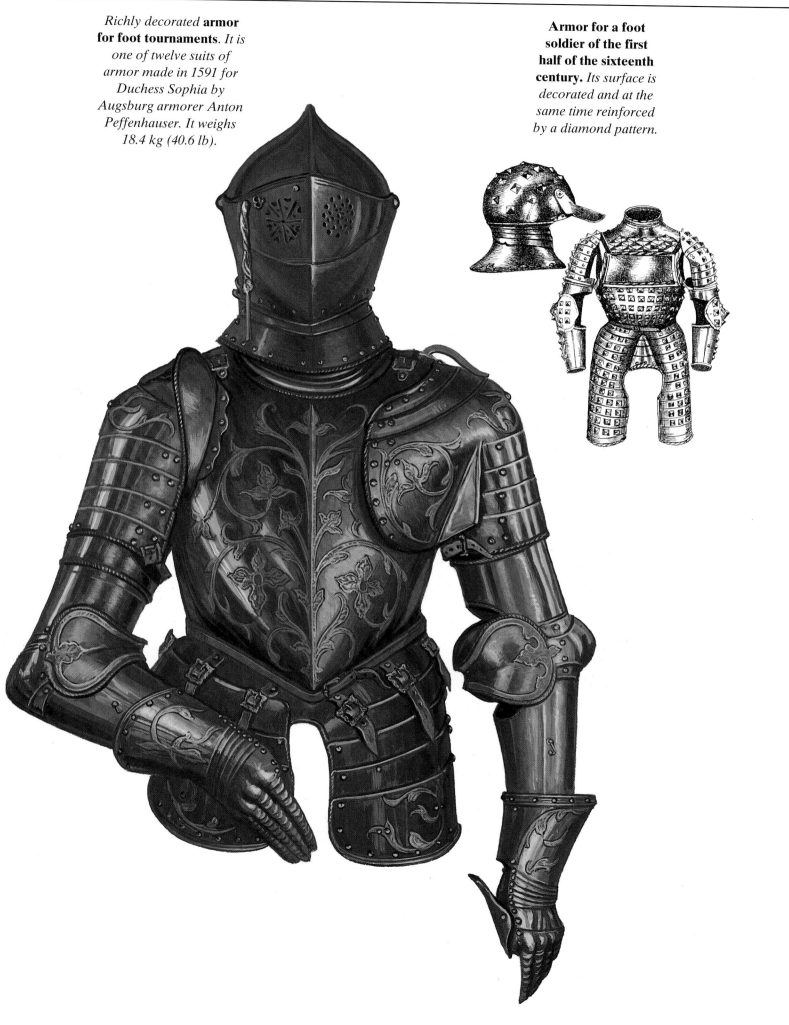

*Richly decorated **armor for foot tournaments**. It is one of twelve suits of armor made in 1591 for Duchess Sophia by Augsburg armorer Anton Peffenhauser. It weighs 18.4 kg (40.6 lb).*

Armor for a foot soldier of the first half of the sixteenth century. *Its surface is decorated and at the same time reinforced by a diamond pattern.*

occasions to display their wealth and social status.

The weaponry of war also changed with the advent of firearms. In the mid-sixteenth century, the number and variety of pieces of armor began to diminish remarkably. Each piece of armor was made more compact and resilient without compromising its craftsmanship or artistry. As the knights found that their legendary courage no longer had a place on the battlefield, they

transferred their skills and their desire to exhibit courage to the arena of the tournament. As mounted knights disappeared from battle, a renaissance in tournament practice began. The tournament became a spectacular theater and was included in all ceremonial occasions of the knightly class. To the tournament of old were added new disciplines full of cunning effects and showmanship. Jousting armor was adapted to match the new tournament style. Armor, as

Italian cuirass from 1570. *A technical masterpiece reflecting the trends of the sixteenth century, it is richly decorated with engraving and gilding.*

Ceremonial armor *made in 1604 by the armorer Heinrich Knopf of Münster. The Duke Johann Georg bought it for 725 gold pieces. The armor, weighing 25.5 kg (56.2 lb), reflects features typical of Flemish-French armor craft.*

before, was created to defend against all types of wounds. As more disciplines were added, so new styles of armor were created.

The need for variation in armor was dealt with quite imaginatively by some countries. By using straps and screws and other fasteners, it was possible to rearrange armor by exchanging or supplementing the entire range of plates as needed. Even with these changes, tournament jousting never became a sport without risk. The French King Henri II himself was mortally wounded during a tournament in the sixteenth century. The number of fatalities from tournaments could not be ignored.

Armor of the sixteenth century reached a new level of craftsmanship. Armorers created masterpieces by solving difficult technological problems and using a whole new range of decorative techniques. Armor reflected the spirit of the era in a truly revolutionary way. Suits of armor became collectors' items. Many collections of armor and masterpieces of weaponry that are famous today date back to the sixteenth century.

It would be rare to find a period more

Morion *of the equipment of the bodyguards of Dukes Christian I and II (1586–1611) of Dresden. The helmet displays the trademark of Nuremberg's armor workshops.*

favorable to the development of armor as art than the sixteenth century. A rare marriage of technique and art existed, with some of the finest artists of the day contributing to masterpieces of armor. Albrecht Dürer himself designed the armor worn by Emperor Maximilian I. Artists as distinguished and varied as Lucas Cranach, the Beham brothers of Germany, Urs Graf and Niklaus Manuel of Switzerland, François Étienne Delaune of France, and goldsmith Eliseus Libaerts of Antwerp designed armor. Famous armor masters founded armor schools. The most famous armor schools were in

Germany, the Tyrol, and Italy. The products from their workshops were exported to royal and princely courts all over Europe.

The German workshops in Nuremberg, Landshut, and Augsburg still enjoyed preeminence. In these workshops, such masters as Martin Oham, Martin Schneider, Anton Peffenhauser or Koloman, and Desiderius Helmschmied honed their skills and produced armor of the highest caliber. In Innsbruck the Seusenhofer family were famous for their first-rate armor products. Milan remained the metropolis of armor craft in Italy. There, first-

Shield *covered in gilded leather, made in Venice in the first half of the sixteenth century.*

rate suits of armor were made by the workshop of the Negrolio family, and one of the most famous Milanese masters was Lucio Piccinino. In France, workshops of that time drew inspiration mainly from Italian models. Armor masters in Fontainebleau made countless complete suits of armor for the French kings of the Valois dynasty, many of which we can admire today in the Musée de l'Armée in Paris. At the end of the sixteenth century, great fame was attained by the armor producers of Greenwich, England.

Over the course of the sixteenth century, both the design of armor and its decoration changed according to fashion. In the 1530s, fluted armor disappeared completely and other excesses, such as unsightly metal flies shaped like erect genitalia, also gradually diminished. The *tapul*, or ridge, a protrusion in the edge of the middle of the front plate was also discarded. Fashion dictated that armor in the Ancient Roman style no longer be made. From the 1560s, front plates were adapted to the Spanish fashion of that time, and were made to look like the coats of civil noble outfits. The *peascod* breastplate was elongated and pointed downward at the waist. Breastplates of this shape were

Richly decorated and gilded **burgonet, made in 1589** *in Augsburg.*

Ornate demi-armor
*made of gilded copper.
It belongs to three suits
of armor made for
Duke Christian I,
Prince Kristian of
Anhalt-Bernburg, and
Duke Johann Georg of
Anhalt-Dessau for
ceremonies which took
place in Dresden in
1590.*

Demi-chamfron, or armored brow-band. *It is a removable piece of equestrian armor. This brow-band, made by Peffenhauser in the 1590s is enameled and decorated with the Saxon coat of arms.*

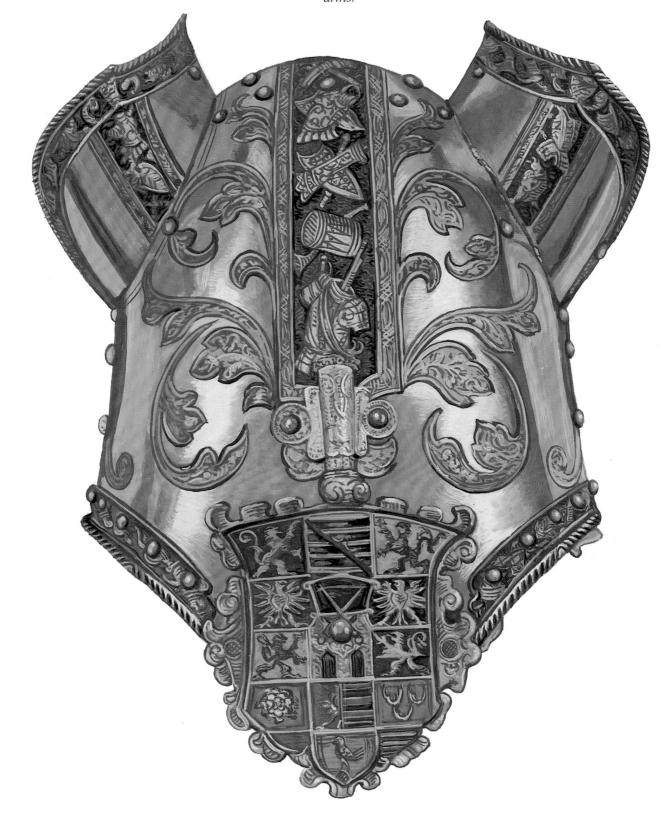

Rich decorations for a man and his horse known as Hercules armor. *It was made in the years 1562–63 in Antwerp. The armor is richly decorated with reliefs of butterflies, griffins, sphinxes, weapons, snakes, dolphins, and grotesque faces. In oval cartouches there are biblical scenes as well as scenes of ancient mythology. Fourteen of these cartouches depict stories about Hercules. The armor was commissioned by King Erik XIV of Sweden.*

We don't know the name of the armorer who forged it, but we know that the designs are those of Étienne Delaune and the goldsmith Eliseus Libaerts.

Opulent armor from the end of the sixteenth century, *made of polished steel in Flanders. The complete suit of armor includes a heavy helmet for the horseman and a forehead plate for the horse.*

used until the beginning of the seventh century.

Techniques for decorating and ornamenting armor reached new heights of excellence. The range of materials was greater than ever before and included iron, steel, copper, bronze, and silver. Plate armor had never been more variously shaped or effusively decorated. It was usually enameled, nielloed, engraved, and etched with bands, and sometimes also covered with relief decoration. Plate armor was first tempered for strength, after which it was ready to be colored and decorated. Motifs of ancient mythology were very popular, especially famous heroes such as Hercules. The biblical heroes

Breastplate *of richly decorated Italian Renaissance armor.*

Samson and David were also common. Anthropomorphous masks became popular in Italian armor schools, while in Germany grotesque masks were fashionable.

No detail was too small to receive artistic attention. Even the tiniest rivet was a masterpiece of workmanship. Fashioned in the shape of a rosette and made of bronze, gold, or silver, the head of the rivet shone out from the surface of the plate. In collections of European armor, we come across dozens of masterpieces from this era. Some of these are illustrated in this chapter. Helmets of this era followed Classical models. While mounted knights of the sixteenth century had virtually no need for shields, they nevertheless continued to be made, and like helmets, they followed ancient models. Shields were painted and round, and covered with flax canvas or gilded leather with ornamentation.

In the seventeenth century, knightly plate

Three-quarter armor from the second half of the sixteenth century made in Innsbruck.

armor gradually fell out of fashion. In armies of that time there was a new kind of cavalry. Mercenary regiments of the regular modern cavalry divided according to roles in battle: a heavy cavalry and a light cavalry. The nobility was usually content with positions of rank in these units, and their armor and equipment was, of course, adapted to their rank. The decorated armor of higher officers could still be made to order, but its design was subordinated to the equipment of the type of cavalry to which the soldier served. Up to the beginning of the eighteenth century, tournament games persisted in various European courts, but they lacked any trace of fighting spirit. Rather, they were expensively organized spectacles in which noblemen showed off their stylized, fantastic costumes and armor. In these tournaments, riders were not really fighting against each other. They attacked inanimate objects, riding at full gallop and using a lance to impale the paper head of a Turk placed on a stake or tear down a hanging metal ring.

The new cavalry still used certain features of defensive protection for the individual. Armor still protected against cuts and thrusts quite

Close jousting helmet *with a mask visor. It is from the period when tournaments were in the decline (the end of the seventeenth century), as reflected in its grotesque appearance and in the less costly material used (bronze).*

The armor of George Clifford, *third earl of Cumberland. It was created by the famous Greenwich school in the third quarter of the sixteenth century.*

Field armor with a close helmet. *The front plate, pointed and shaped in the peasecod style, reflects the fashion of the 1570s. The armor is the work of German armorers.*

Gilded and enameled morion,
belonging to a complete suit of armor. The suit included a similarly decorated shield made by French armorers for King Charles IX.

satisfactorily, so it was only necessary to eliminate superfluous plates and reduce the armor to a bare minimum. The semiheavy cavalry of the sixteenth century wore, for example, *trabant* or three-quarter armor, which consisted of the *morion,* or a version of the open-faced helmet known as the *burgonet,* cuirass (i.e., front and back plate), skirt and armor tassets reaching to the knees (or shorter). From the knees down, the rider was protected only by high riding boots. His arms were covered by several overlapping plates reaching from the shoulder to the elbow, and possibly by chain sleeves.

In the seventeenth century, components of protective armor were only used by certain kinds of cavalry, mainly cuirassiers. The typical cuirassier's armor of the first half of the seventeenth century consisted of a *close helmet* with a long bill and a movable visor. This visor was either solid, with slits for eyes and airholes (as on former knightly helmets), or it could be a grid or series of bars. Protection for the neck was provided by a *gorget,* a plate which was worn under the cuirass (front and back plates). The arms were covered all around by plates; the hands were covered by metal gauntlets. Wide, long tassets reaching from the rider's waist to his knees were made from many overlapping plates decorated with rivets. In central Europe, such

Jousting helmet *for mounted tilting made for Emperor Maximilian II by Saxon armorers around 1560.*

The armor of English King Henry VIII, made in the 1540s, *probably by French armorers.*

armor was blackened, and officers' cuirasses were decorated with blackened rivets with gilded or copper heads. The most noticeable feature of armor was its completely new design. The front plate lacked the distinctive central edge. It was much shorter, giving the figure the impression of having a short trunk and wide leggings. In fact, this design imitated the civil garment of that time. As for the equipment of cuirassiers, close helmets were gradually replaced by lighter helmets, called *pappenheim,* or lobster-tailed, helmets. Influenced in design by the Orient, the pappenheim had an oblong or slightly conical skull, the end of which was formed by a flat edge along the ear level. The sides of the head were protected by movable hanging cheek plates that

Close helmet *from the jousting armor of French King Francis I. It was made in the workshop of Innsbruck's master armorer Georg Seusenhofer in 1539–40. Its decoration comes from the workshop of Degen Pirger.*

clasped under the chin. The back of the neck was covered by a wide and relatively long protective piece consisting of many overlapping metal plates. The helmet retained the typical long bill, into which a movable nasal was set.

Infantry played a central role in battles of the sixteenth century. At first, foot soldiers retained their armor. The armor of foot soldiers was light and seemingly did not hamper the freedom of movement necessary for battle. For example, landsknechts wore front and sometimes even back plates and longer tassets extending from the thigh to just above the knee. The most vulnerable soldiers were those in the front lines, and they wore full plate armor which also covered the arms. The infantry also wore

Burgonet *with a central ridge, armored bill, and movable cheek plates. The helmet, probably made by Landshut armorer Sigmund Wolf in 1560, is part of the field armor of Duke Johann Wilhelm of Weimar.*

helmets. The plain, pointed "musketeer" helmet was the type most often worn by the infantry. It was made of metal or hard leather, and was supplemented by the morion helmet. Over the course of the sixteenth century, the roles of the infantry became specialized, and an infantry unit was usually made up of two kinds of foot soldiers. The first kind were musketeers, who usually didn't wear any armor except morions or fusilier schischaks. The second kind were pikemen, who had a more difficult role. It was mainly the pikemen who had to enter into one-on-one combat. In addition, they had to protect the musketeers well, not only when the musketeers were engaged in attack, but any time they undertook the lengthy process of reloading their weapons, at which point the musketeers were almost defenseless. Therefore, it was

Classical-style **burgonet**
made in Milan between
1550–1570. Its creator was
probably Lucio Piccinino.

Richly decorated relief
Renaissance shield
(sixteenth century).

Three-quarter, **richly decorated cuirassier's armor** *belonging to the Duke of Savoy. It was made in northern Italy around 1620.*

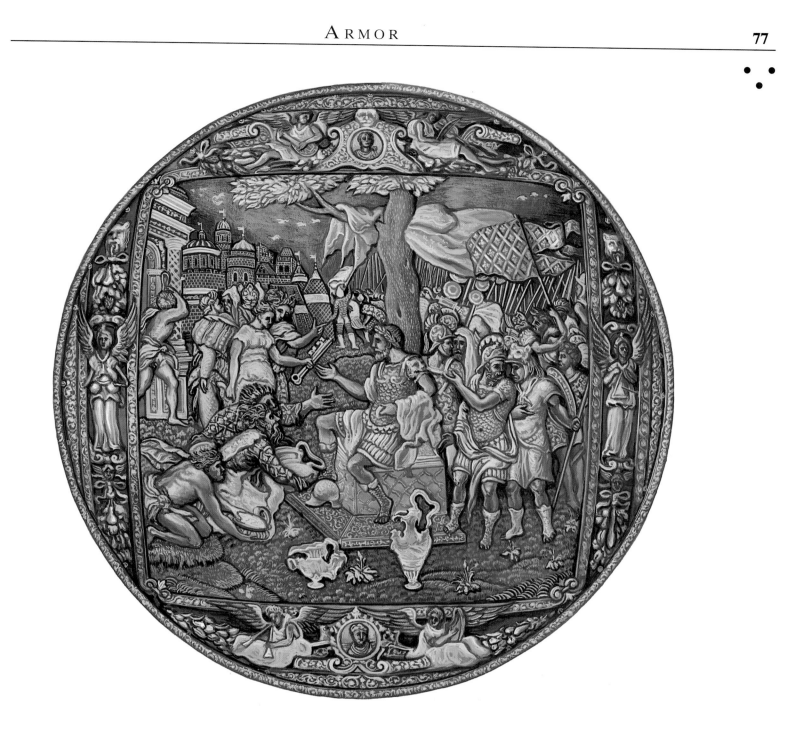

*Round, richly decorated
Renaissance* **shield.** *It
originates from the workshop
of the Milanese master Lucio
Piccinino (before 1567).*

Cuirassier's steel three-quarter armor. *The product of Italian or German armorers from the first half of the seventeenth century, the complete armor weighs 27.3 kg (60.2 lb).*

Richly decorated three-quarter armor of the second half of the seventeenth century. *Blackened and decorated with gilded engraving, it was probably made in central Europe for a high military officer.*

necessary that pikemen wear armor. The pikeman's armor included a helmet, cuirass, and very wide, long tassets.

Pikemen became the last foot soldiers to wear protective armor in western and central Europe. The centralization of armies and their transition to mercenary armies brought an end to the armor craft. For numerous regiments of mercenary armies, more basic armor was made by manufacturers who could supply enough equipment at an acceptable price. Radical changes in military practice — most notably, the use of firearms — rendered protective armor obsolete.

Pear-shaped, richly decorated **musketeer helmet**
*with narrow brim, made in northern
Italy at the end of the sixteenth
century.*

Lobster-tailed helmet, cuirass, protection for the bridle arm and buff coat. *This cuirassier's equipment is typical of English cuirasses of the second half of the seventeenth century. The complete suit of armor belonged to King James II.*

**Cuirassier of the
seventeenth century** *in a full
suit of armor, accurately
modeled in miniature.*

Cuirassier's blackened armor from the second half of the seventeenth century.
The armor belonged to Count Sporck.

Classical style burgonet
made in Augsburg
before 1603.

Eagle helmet, *made of gilded copper and decorated with colored glass. It formed a pair together with a decorated fist shield. In 1709 it was used during the ring tournament of Danish King Frederick IV.*

Pappenheim or lobster-tailed helmet from the second half of the seventeenth century. *The surface of the helmet is blackened, engraved, with remains of gilding. It has a movable three-piece neck guard, cut cheek plates, and a star pattern of holes for hearing.*

Musketeer helmet.
*This helmet was made of leather
in Italy at the end of the sixteenth
century.*

BETWEEN THE ORIENT
AND EUROPE

A book about the history of armor would not be complete if it did not cover the nations of central and eastern Europe, particularly Russia, Hungary, and Poland. Because of their location, these countries were influenced not only by the cultures of the West but also those of the Byzantine Empire and the Orient. In the marketplaces of eastern and central Europe, products from the Orient and from western Europe could be found side by side. This cross-pollination of influence affected all areas of life, and the development of armor was no exception.

The armies of eastern and central Europe had to defend against invasions from the Mongol and Turco-Tatars as well as the military forces of the Ottoman Turks. In order to survive, the armies in the region had to be prepared for a wide variety of fighting styles and equipment. Armor of the soldiers was therefore varied, both in its components and decorative styles. Armor was also influenced by local and national traditions.

In the tenth century, nomadic tribes from Hungary launched their brutal attacks on central Europe. Countless victims were lost in the eventually successful defense. The Hungarian invaders protected themselves by wearing bronze helmets or rich, felt caps reinforced with mounting; leather or felt caftans, richly quilted with small plates and buttons of bronze, copper, or silver; and smaller ringed wooden shields covered with leather.

After the settlement of the Hungarians in the Danube region, and their development as a nation and their Christianization, Hungarian soldiers were often in contact with western and central Europe. Due to this constant contact, Hungarian nobility adopted the western style of armor and went into battle equipped in the same way as other European knights. A group called the Cumans settled in Hungary and fought and armored themselves like nomadic cavalry. Their protection in battle consisted of round shields, short chain tunics, and spiked conical helmets.

Hussar helmet of the kettle hat style. *This helmet, from the second half of the sixteenth century, provided a neck guard, cheek plates, and a nasal.*

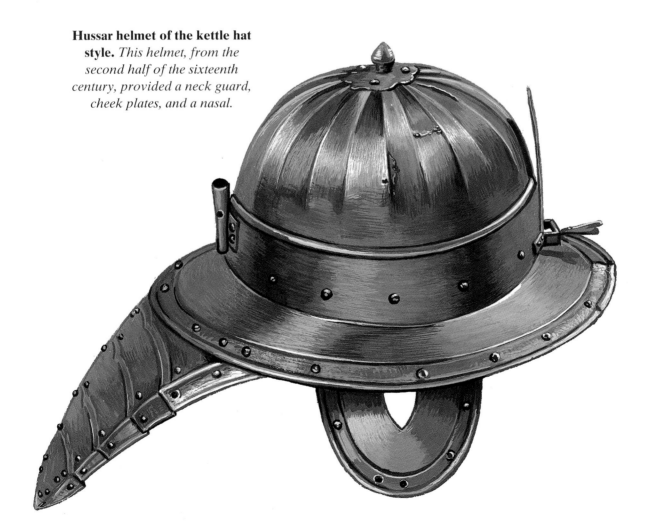

Hungarian hussar demi-armor from the end of the sixteenth century. *It consists of a burgonet with a movable nasal, a chain kilt, and a "crawfish" (band) cuirass.*

In the fourteenth century, when the Ottoman Turks penetrated the Balkans, the Hungarian state was soon in serious danger. For several centuries central Europe had been defending against Turkish expansion with great difficulty and at the cost of many lives. Long-term, direct contact with the Turkish forces influenced the equipment of Hungarian soldiers. The most prevalent type of soldier in the Hungarian army was the hussar, a light cavalryman with arms and armor similar to the Turkish *deli*. The hussar wore a *dolman,* or fur-lined jacket, boots extending to midcalf, and a cap consisting of a *kolpak,* or fur covering around a cylindrical hat. A Hungarian riding shield offered to the hussar additional protection. Shaped like either an asymmetrical square or a wing, the wooden shield was covered by parchment and sometimes furnished with a slit in which a lance could be placed. Semiheavy cavalry wore chain tunics, sometimes reinforced with interwoven plates, or semiarmor plate. Plate cuirasses, called *crawfish,* became popular. These were pulled over chain mail, the style of which was probably

Breastplate of hussar cuirass from the end of the sixteenth century.
It is a Hungarian crawfish cuirass made of eight bands.

influenced by the light, trabant armor worn by Italian and German mercenaries in the sixteenth century. Hungarian pointed helmets of the "musketeer" style were in widespread use and, to a great extent, the Turkish *turban helmet* was imitated. The turban helmet had an onion-shaped skull, a long bill, ear protectors, a shorter, movable pendant neck guard, and a sliding nasal. Because many helmets for Oriental armies were made by craftsmen in western Europe, the Turkish turban helmet in turn influenced western helmet styles. German

Hungarian burgonet,
*influenced by Oriental helmets.
It has a small bill, a sliding
nasal, pendant cheek plates,
and a neck guard.*

settlers in Transylvania played the most important role in influencing the development of Hungarian national armor in the sixteenth and seventeenth centuries.

The Polish state was greatly influenced by its connections with the Holy Roman Empire and the Vikings, as well as its neighbors on the eastern border, the Kievan Russ. Several helmets of Russian origin have been found in Poland. Experts speculate that they were either the spoils of plunder or imported through trade with Kiev. For the most part, however, Poland's predominant influence came from the West. Polish knights, with very few exceptions,

Hussar burgonet, *a pointed helmet from the mid-eighteenth century. Made of two richly decorated plates and weighing 2.28 kg (5 lb), the helmet probably belonged to Dominik Aleksandrowicz Petyhorski, a lieutenant of the Lithuanian division.*

wore knightly armor that any European knight would have. This was not the case in the Grand Duchy of Lithuania, which had been annexed to Poland by a royal marriage in the fourteenth century. Lithuanian boyars used, apart from chain armor, Russian-style plate coats. Their helmets were high-pointed kettle hats. The shield of the Lithuanian boyar was usually a small, wooden riding pavis, which protected the rider well and was relatively light and easy to manipulate. It is interesting to note that like the Lithuanians, the Teutonic Knights also used the riding pavis for protection.

From the sixteenth century on, the state of Poland encountered the Russians, the Tatars, and the Turks on the battlefield. This required that the armor of the Poles became more varied. Polish nobility continued to commission western European-style armor, but were also known to wear armor imported from the Orient. The Polish army consisted of ethnic groups as diverse as Tatars, Cossacks, Polish nobles, and western European mercenaries. Gradually, an armor that reflected Poland's national character was forged: the armor of the Polish hussars. The elite of the Polish army, the Polish hussars were especially prestigious in the seventeenth century.

Gilded Polish **burgonet,** *a pointed variant from the second half of the sixteenth century.*

Russian plate armor of the Byzantine-Oriental style. *In an earlier version, the plates were joined with a strap; later they were fastened to a cloth or leather garment.*

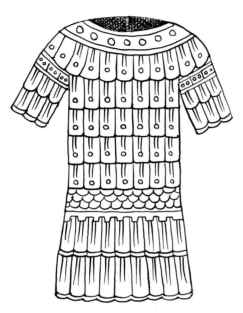

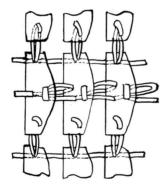

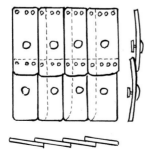

Bachterets, *made in Poznan, circa 1580.*

Hussar bastard armor, *made in Poland at the turn of the sixteenth and seventeenth centuries. It is made with copper rivets. The armor weighs 12.5 kg (27.6 lb); the helmet, 2.23 kg (4.9 lb).*

Armor of the Polish hussars included a helmet, cuirass, gorget, pauldrons, coverings for the upper arms, *pasguards,* and, in some cases, plate coverings for the legs from waist to knee as well. The helmet of hussar armor underwent a long evolution. At first, Polish hussars used western European-style iron hats with movable ear protectors and a metal neck guard (two influences from the Oriental helmet). Later, depending on the era, hussar pointed helmets with semicircular, or slightly conical skulls were the most popular helmet of the

Polish hussars. The skull included a long bill, ear protectors, a neck guard, and a movable nasal. The helmet was usually richly decorated. The cuirass of hussar armor consisted of a front plate (made of many pieces) and sometimes, a back plate. The front plate was often decorated with a knight's cross and a cartouche of the Virgin Mary. Shoulder straps were attached to the collar of the armor and were followed by plate protection for the upper part of the arm. The forearms and elbows were protected by pasguards of the Oriental type. The

Breastplate *of hussar armor from the first half of the seventeenth century. It is decorated with a knight's cross and a cartouche of the Virgin Mary.*

decoration was made of rivet heads, rosettes, and so on.

So-called *bastard armor* was also quite common. This western European armor was arranged so that it would fit the standard of Polish hussar armor. In examining this armor, we can find older Renaissance breastplates with a distinct central edge, tapul, or peasecod. Unique features of hussar armor included "wings" attached to the saddle or to the back plate of armor. These wings were wooden laths, about 110–120 cm (42.9–46.8 in) long, forming

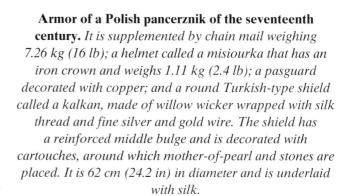

Armor of a Polish pancerznik of the seventeenth century. *It is supplemented by chain mail weighing 7.26 kg (16 lb); a helmet called a misiourka that has an iron crown and weighs 1.11 kg (2.4 lb); a pasguard decorated with copper; and a round Turkish-type shield called a kalkan, made of willow wicker wrapped with silk thread and fine silver and gold wire. The shield has a reinforced middle bulge and is decorated with cartouches, around which mother-of-pearl and stones are placed. It is 62 cm (24.2 in) in diameter and is underlaid with silk.*

a massive arch above the hussar's head and densely decorated with crane or falcon feathers. A hussar with wings above his head presented a threatening appearance to his opponent. The sound made by the wings of a rider in motion frightened the horses of his enemies, and the laths stretching out and forming a massive arch over his head prevented him from being caught with a Tatar lasso. Hussar armor protected well against cuts and thrusts, and at the same time it was fairly light, weighing about 15 kg (33.1 lb). The wings weighed about 0.5 kg (1.1 lb).

Armor should be light and should protect only the most vulnerable parts of the body against cuts and blows. To a certain extent, hussar armor fulfilled these demands. Paradoxically, as a reflection of knighthood, the desire for a showy appearance brought to Polish battlefields *jazerants* — scaled armor made of relatively small metal scales attached to a cloth or leather garment. The shape of jazerants varied. They appeared either as short-sleeved, waist-length vests or as armor covering the whole soldier's body. Jazerant parts could also be combined with plate or chain armor. This was supplemented by a helmet, also made of scales attached to leather. The helmet was either in the shape of the hussar basinet or wrapped with

Breastplate of hussar armor from the first half of the eighteenth century, *made of polished steel and lined on the inside with velvet. It belonged to a member of the Radziwill retinue, which is clear from the decoration of the Radziwill coat of arms.*

a colored turban. Jazerant armor was by no means practical. It didn't provide more protection than hussar armor, and at the same time it was much heavier, weighing more than 25 kg (55 lb). In spite of these disadvantages, it remained popular in Poland for a long time, until around the middle of the eighteenth century.

The special semiheavy cavalry in Poland were called the *pancerznik*. They were named after their armor, a chain tunic called *pancerz* (mail). The tunic weighed 4.5–10 kg (9.9–22 lb), depending on the size of the chains of which it was made, which often were 8–10 mm (0.3–0.4 in.) in diameter. The forearm was usually protected by Oriental pasguards, while the head was covered by a *misiourka*. The equipment also included a shield – the Oriental round *kalkan*, or mail hood with plate top.

For centuries, foot soldiers made up the armies of Russian countries. In the second half of the tenth century, after several clashes with nomads, Russian princes established a cavalry. Russian armor was greatly influenced by the Byzantine Empire as well as by Russia's neighbors, the Vikings (or Varangians). Until the eleventh century, the basic armor consisted

Janissary kolpak *of copper and silvered plate. Weighing 1.5 kg (3.3 lb) and made of four pieces, this type of kolpak was worn by janissaries of King Augustus II of Poland. It was popular in the 1730s.*

Jazerant turban helmet from the seventeenth century. *Such helmets were worn by Polish fighters together with jazerant (scaled) armor. The helmet consists of a leather cap with riveted metal scales, wrapped with a silk turban.*

Pauldron and pasguard *of hussar armor of Dominik Aleksandrowicz, decorated with gilded copper, circa 1765.*

Polish jazerant (scaled) demi-armor from the turn of the seventeenth and eighteenth centuries. *It is decorated with a gilded copper epaulet on the shoulder and pauldrons on which there are gilded copper grotesque faces. It is lined with velvet and leather.*

Hussar armor from the second half of the seventeenth century *made of polished iron with copper ornamentation. There are typical "wings" attached to the back side; the laths of the wings are made of wood.*

of a large, round shield that covered the upper half of the soldier's body. This armor was the only armor available to most Russian soldiers. Wealthier members of the retinue wore short-sleeved chain tunics or plate mail of the Byzantine Empire. This plate mail was made of oblong plates tied together with straps. Additionally, wealthy soldiers wore a helmet unfamiliar to western Europe. Adapted from Asian helmets, the Russian helmet was made of several plates that were fastened to one another, embossed, and elongated conically to form a high spike at the top. A chain veil, called a *barmice,* attached to the edge of the

helmet greatly improved the helmet's protection.

In the eleventh century, plate and chain armor predominated. Both were shaped like a short-sleeved coat ending below the soldier's loins. The typical Russian helmet just described was worn, supplemented by a kite-shaped shield typical of other parts of Europe. Wooden and covered with leather, the shield had reinforced edges and its center was reinforced.

In the twelfth century, scaled outfits in the same form as the armor just described appeared in Russia. Scales, not all of the same size, were fastened to a leather garment. The size of scaled outfits varied. Some covered just the

Royal crowns *also usually had the character of helmets. This is a "cap" of Prince Vladimir II. A manuscript from the early twelfth century illustrates this.*

Conical helmet *made of one piece of metal. There is a nasal attached to the lower edge, and a reinforced brim above the eyes. The eyelets for fastening a chain veil, or barmice, are preserved on the nasal.*

A silver-covered plate with a relief picture of the archangel Michael is attached to the forehead piece. The spike of the helmet is decorated with a silver canopy with a picture of Saint George, Saint Basil, Christ Pantocrator, and Saint Theodore. The helmet's lower edge is decorated with a gilded silver band with relief ornamentation. The helmet dates from the 1210s and is ascribed to Prince Yaroslav Vsevolodovich of Kiev.

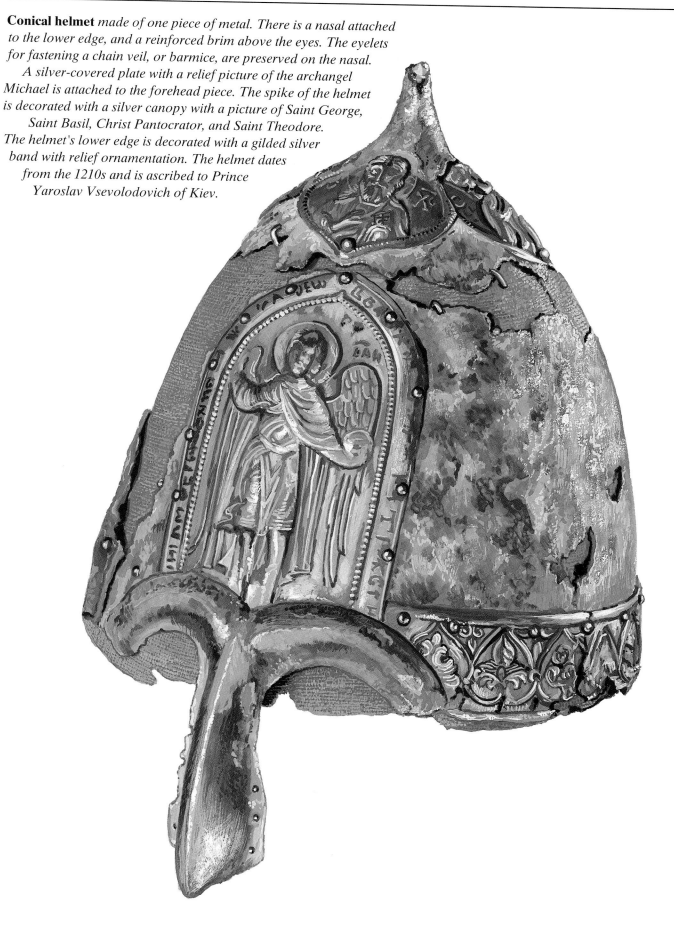

soldier's trunk, while longer ones included sleeves and extended to the loins. This armor was sufficient for protection against the cuts and arrow wounds of the enemy, and was light enough so as not to hinder movement.

At the turn of the twelfth and thirteenth centuries, Russian principalities were attacked by the Teutonic Knights from the northeast. Perhaps influenced by their experience fighting the well-armored heavy infantry of western Europe, Russian mounted soldiers completely covered themselves in armor in the fight against the Teutonic Knights. The Russian soldiers wore long-sleeved, knee-length chain tunics, and their legs were covered in chain stockings. Their heads were protected by conical helmets with a nasal or shade, which protected the upper part of the face. A kite-shaped shield completed the armor. While Byzantine plate armor was still in use in Russia, it was much improved. Plates of different shapes and thickness were attached in an overlapping manner to a cloth or leather garment. This style of armor remained popular in Russia until the fifteenth century.

Mongolian invasions and conflicts with Turks and Lithuanians led to many changes in Russian armor in the fourteenth and fifteenth centuries. Round shields returned to the battlefield in

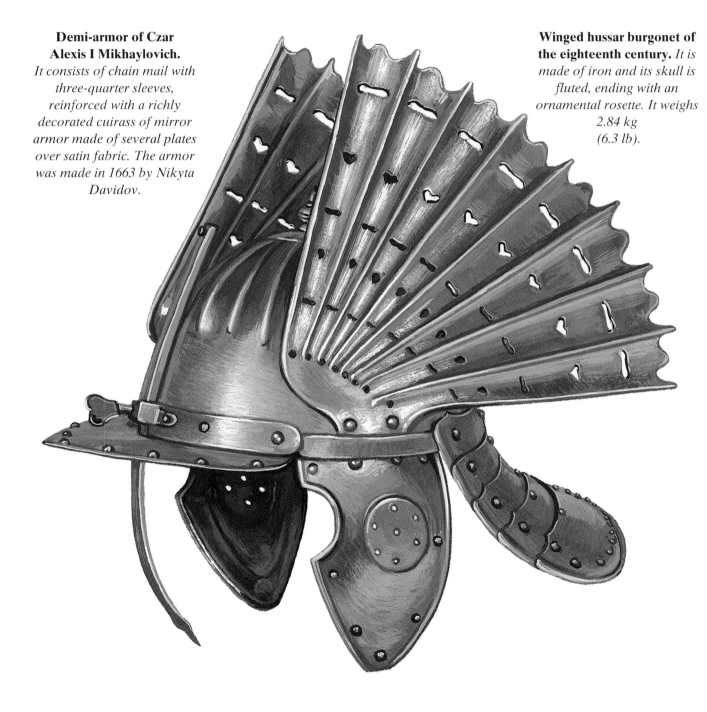

Demi-armor of Czar Alexis I Mikhaylovich. *It consists of chain mail with three-quarter sleeves, reinforced with a richly decorated cuirass of mirror armor made of several plates over satin fabric. The armor was made in 1663 by Nikyta Davidov.*

Winged hussar burgonet of the eighteenth century. *It is made of iron and its skull is fluted, ending with an ornamental rosette. It weighs 2.84 kg (6.3 lb).*

**Breastplate of a cuirass from the
second half of the seventeenth century.**
*It is decorated with rich, floral
ornamentation with a cartouche on
which are visible a lion with a sword
and a bunch of arrows.*

**A pair of vambraces (forearm guards)
from the seventeenth century.** *Each
consists of three pieces joined with chain
links. The combination of small plates
and chains forms the bachterets.*

place of the kite-shaped shield. Triangular shields, adapted from western European knightly armor, were also used. While the helmet was still conical the equipment now included pointed helmets with bills, ear protectors, and neck guards in imitation of Oriental models.

Some of the most interesting changes to Russian armor were the result of Persian and Turkish influences. A whole range of armor appeared in which the chain mail was combined with plates. One type of armor was the *colontar,* which was sleeveless and boasted back and breast pieces clasped at the hips. Each piece was made of bigger metal plates connected by chain links. From Persia *bachterets* (*begter* in Persian) came to Russia, an outfit made of thick vertical bands of oblong plates joined to a chain framework so that they would overlap. These pieces of armor consisted of metal plates connected to chain links. There were as many as fifteen hundred plates, and the armor weighed about 12 kg (26.5 lb). The colontar provided high-quality protection and unlimited mobility. The *kujak,* a variation on the western European brigandine, was worn over chain mail. Russian writings of 1548 give the earliest record of the *jushman,* chain mail with a row of plates attached between chain links (up to dozens of plates). The armor weighed as much as 15 kg (33.1 lb), and the

Typical bachterets or combination armor. *Made by the armorer Konon Mikhailov for Emperor Mikhail Fyodorovich in 1620. It is made of steel plates and rings, and decorated with golden rosettes.*

plates were silvered and gilded. Perhaps the most stunning innovation in Russian armor was the *baidan,* chain mail made of large, flat chains, which protected against cuts extremely well. *Mirrors* (in Persian, *chair aina*), or reinforcing plates, were of Persian origin. Originally there were four mirrors — one back plate, one breastplate, and two side plates — were joined together with a set of straps and buckles. The name was derived from the fact that these plates were polished until they shone like mirrors. Later, in the seventeenth century, mirrors became small masterpieces in Russia. Plates or mirrors were attached to expensive fabrics; their shape, number, and decoration changed, and the whole mirror was used to form a sort of plate-covered vest. Horses of the Russian heavy cavalry were protected by armor inspired by Oriental models. The *chaldar* — a caparison covered by richly decorated plates of various shapes and

dimensions — covered the horse's chest, hips, and rump.

In Russia, *soft armor* (i.e., armor made of nonmetallic materials) was also quite common. Soft armor consisted of padded or quilted cotton kaftans supplemented by similarly constructed headgear. A typical feature was a quilted high-standing collar protecting the nape of the neck. This type of armor provided satisfactory protection against arrow wounds and cuts, and was an affordable and welcome armor for the poorer members of the army.

Between the second half of the seventeenth century and the beginning of the eighteenth century, Russian "national" armor gradually vanished. Czar Peter I wanted the Russian army to emulate as quickly as possible the western European standard of the time, both in training and fighting tactics and in the equipment and armor. Variety disappeared and Russian armor became standardized.

Round iron shield *decorated with a relief of the cross and bronze rivets. It is 52 cm (20.3 in.) in diameter and dates from the seventeenth century.*

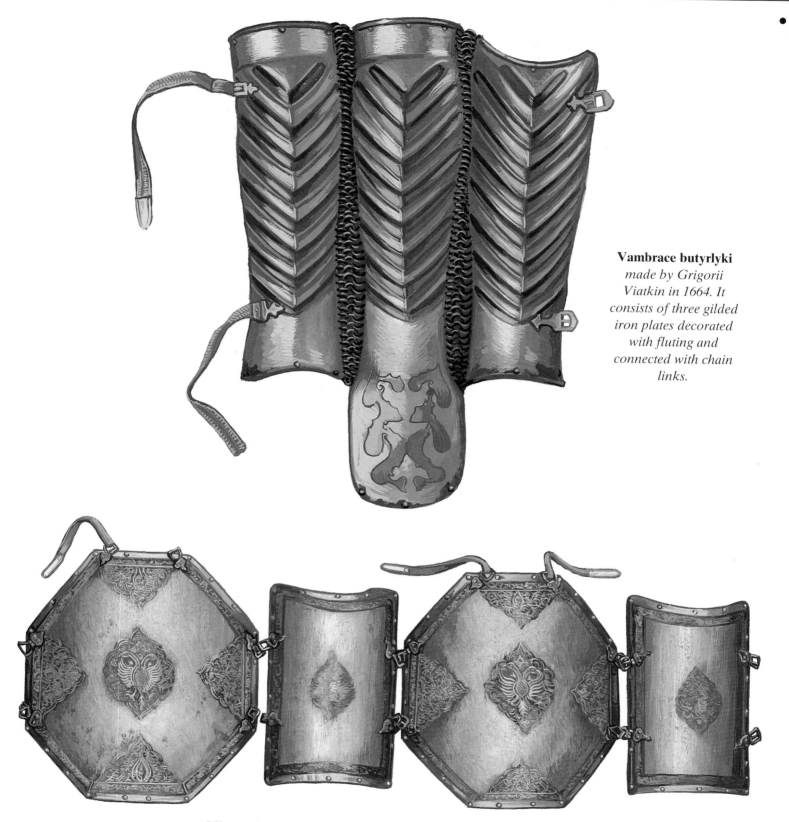

Vambrace butyrlyki *made by Grigorii Viatkin in 1664. It consists of three gilded iron plates decorated with fluting and connected with chain links.*

Mirror plate armor. *This type of reinforcing armor is derived from Persian patterns. It was forged in the seventeenth century of steel and decorated with floral ornamentation and central cartouches of a czar's two-headed eagle.*

THE WEAPONS OF
THE ORIENT

Europeans associate the Orient with exotic, faraway places. The Orient can be defined geographically in several ways. We can narrow the term to the Islamic countries of the Near East or the states of the Far East. We can identify the entire continent of Asia as the Orient or apply the term only to certain territories within that huge continent. A book of this size cannot possibly attempt to include all the variety and complexity of the armor used in continental Asia over many centuries. Instead, we will concentrate on certain regions of particular interest.

When the Western Roman Empire

Reinforced plates *of the type, worn over chain armor, that were used in Persia. There were four plates (in Persian,* **chair aina***). They were joined together by straps or metal covered with small bands of mail. The plate in the picture is decorated by damascening and gilding.*

Lacquered vambrace (armguard) *dastan connected with a glove quilted with chain links. It is covered by gold and silver decoration imitating damascene, and the inner side is padded with velvet. The warrior attached it to his forearm with straps.*

disintegrated, Europe started many aspects of its civilization over again. The art and technique of fighting changed in the Western Roman Empire, influenced by the decline of armor production. New types of armor came into existence to fill the need. This break with tradition where armor is concerned did not happen in the Near East, where the Byzantine Empire was expanding. While the Western Roman Empire fell apart, the Eastern Roman Empire (i.e., the Byzantine Empire) flourished. Craftsmen working in Eastern Roman towns were able to maintain and improve ancient technologies for creating armor. Frequent battles with soldiers of various Asian states and hordes of Asian invaders contributed

to the cultural cross-pollination between the Eastern Roman Empire and the Orient. Naturally, this influence also affected the evolution of armor.

In ancient times, the most important centers of development and production of armor were in the territory of Syria, formerly the Assyrian Empire, particularly in Persia. Until the seventh century, Sassanian Persia was a cultural melting pot; consequently, its armor production reflected centuries of Islamic craftsmanship.

The Persians relied on heavy cavalry for success in battle. The cavalryman wore a knee-length coat, the surface of which was covered with metal scales or closely connected plates.

Round shield *made of steel in the nineteenth century. Shields of this type were used by Indian and Persian soldiers. Called a* **dhal** *or* **sipar,** *this shield is decorated with gilding. Grips for the warrior's left hand, which are on the inner side of the shield, are covered from the outer side with a massive metal bulge.*

This outfit fastened at the back. Its short sleeves covered the arms to the elbows, and in order to protect the forearms and the elbow joint, the Persians created a specific plate called the *bazuband.*

Up until the nineteenth century, the horseman wore a conical helmet, similar in shape to that worn by Assyrian soldiers, but with spikes. It was sometimes made with several interconnecting plates that were fastened to each other or to metal ribs. Attached to the helmet was a plate or

War elephant of India, *head covered with metal plates and a caparison braced by iron plates.*

Richly decorated Turkish **turban helmet with a veil of metal plates** *connected by chain links. It originates from the fifteenth century.*

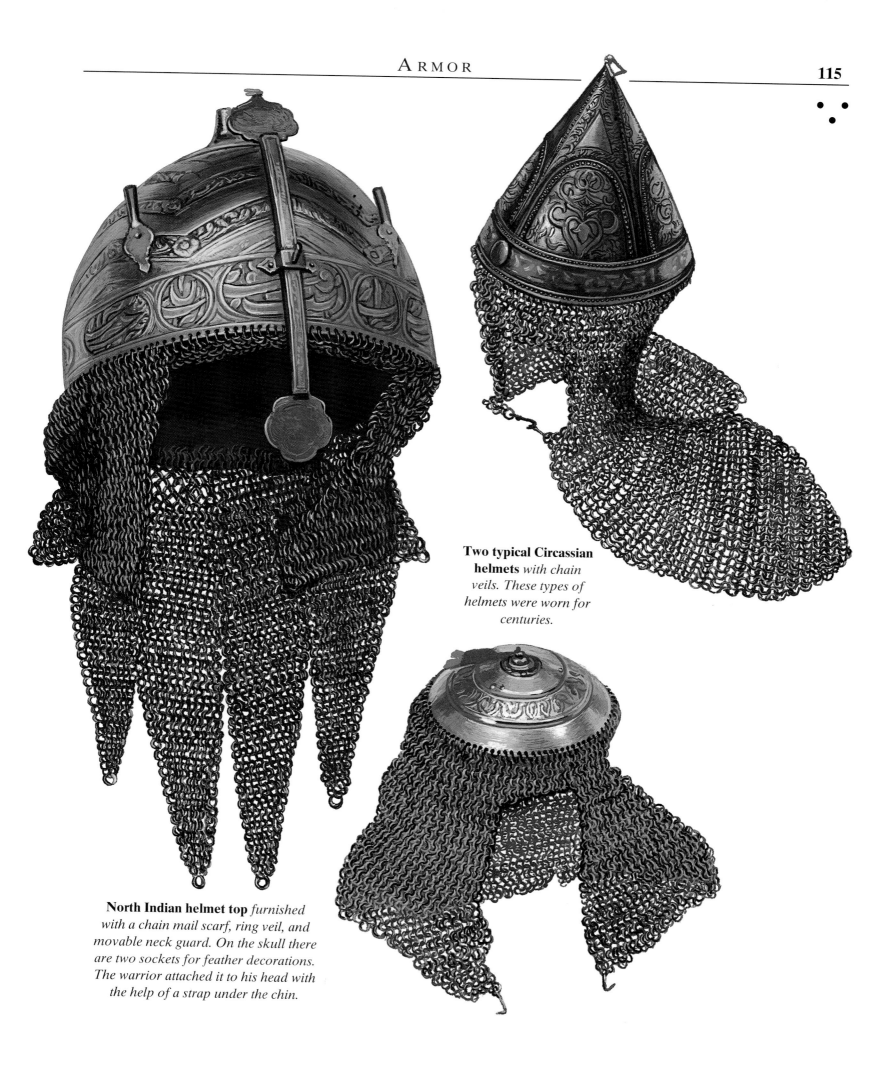

Two typical Circassian helmets *with chain veils. These types of helmets were worn for centuries.*

North Indian helmet top *furnished with a chain mail scarf, ring veil, and movable neck guard. On the skull there are two sockets for feather decorations. The warrior attached it to his head with the help of a strap under the chin.*

scaled veil, which protected the back of the neck, the neck itself, and the soldier's shoulders. Chain armor, which came to the Near East as a result of battles with the Romans, was a major innovation in Oriental armor. Invented by Celts, chain armor became the most common kind of protective armor in Asia. This armor was so versatile that it served not only the heavy cavalry serving in the newly forming states in the Middle East at that time, but also the mounted soldiers who played a crucial role in the nomadic Turco-Tatar tribes to the east of the Volga River.

When the Arabs began their invasions in the seventh century, their army consisted of light cavalry whose major protection came from round shields. After battles with the Persians and the Byzantines, they gradually wore more sophisticated armor, the basis of which was a chain mail with spiked helmet. Mameluke, Turkish, and Circassian elite mercenary troops in the service of the Egyptian sultan brought with them advanced and varied armor. So strong was their influence that they are said to have played a role in the creation of the typical Oriental "turban helmet." In fact, this helmet developed from Persian models. Massive and spiked with an onion-shaped skull, the turban helmet came in two styles. To one, a chain veil was added. The other combined the Persian and Roman helmet traditions. The onion-shaped pointed helmet boasted movable pendant metal protectors for the ears and sides of the face. This feature was

Circassian vambrace and gloves *covered with chain mail from the turn of the eighteenth and nineteenth centuries.*

really a modification of the cheek plates of Roman helmets. Other innovations of the onion helmet were a metal bill, a metal nasal that went through the bill, and neck guards. When Ottoman Turks invaded Hungary, Poland, and Russia in the sixteenth and seventeenth centuries, this helmet became famous in those countries and eventually throughout the whole of Europe. Chain mail also went through some changes. Following Persian style, different-sized plates were placed into the mail for reinforcement. The result could be mail with vertically arranged metal plates, called a *sjawskah,* or a tunic strengthened with a plate band, called a *zirah baktar.*

The onslaught of the Mongols brought influences rooted in the Chinese culture as well as in the Middle East. Most notable among these influences was the protective armor specific to the Far East as well as to Persia and Afghanistan. This armor boasted a helmet with several metal plates or scales, and included chain mail as well as plate coats. In fact, these were Oriental imitations of brigandine. Large metal plates fastened onto the armor doubled the protection of the breast and back. These plates were called *chair aina,* which in Persian means "four mirrors." They were so called because they were polished until they shone like a mirror, then decorated with gold and silver. The soldier's forearms were protected by lacquered plates or bazubands, and the horseman's legs

Samurai heavy helmet, *hoshi-kabuto, with its extra reinforcement, belonging to a warrior of the Taira dynasty. The skull, fastened up by many plates, dates from the fifteenth century. The helmet shown is from the eighteenth century.*

Typical Indian (Sind) armor from the eighteenth century. *The helmet is made of steel and decorated with bronze. The covering of the body includes bronze plates connected by chain links.*

Luxurious Chinese brigandine.

were covered in leather or cloth with quilted metal knee pieces covered by smaller metal plates. These coverings, attached to the soldier's trousers, reached to just below the knees. As in other Islamic regions, the shield was round.

From the sixteenth to the nineteenth century, the five-piece suit of armor was the standard in Persia. The helmet had a narrow, semicircular skull, and its shape became more square. A movable nasal protected the face and was attached to two metal sockets to be decorated with feathers. Additionally, the chain veil reached the shoulders while chain mail extended to the middle of the thighs. An ornament was sometimes formed by combining rings of various materials — steel, copper, or even bronze — on chain mail. Mail was supplemented by some plate pieces such as vambraces and mirrors, which were mostly made of high-quality Damascus steel covered with rich ornamental decoration.

Turkey influenced the armor of eastern and central Europe quite significantly. Through centuries of Turkish attacks on Christian Europe, much was learned from the formidable Turkish army, including advances in armor. Master armor craftsmen from all over the world, including Persians, Syrians, Armenians, Greeks, Hungarians, and Italians, worked in Istanbul's workshops and armories.

The Turks were most noted for their elite infantry, known as the *janissaries,* who wore no protective armor. However, the Turkish cavalry, especially the *Sipahi,* did use protective armor. The cavalry equipment included chain mail or sometimes a chain framework combined with metal plates. Persian mirrors were very popular in Turkey, but they were not fastened by straps. Rather, plates were attached to a vest and reinforced with other metal plates. The legs of the Turkish mounted soldiers were protected by chain hose, which also had metal plates inserted into a chain framework. Three types of helmets were used: the turban pointed helm; the onion helmet, with ear protectors, neck guard, and bill; and the misiourka. Since the fifteenth century, this light helmet, consisting of a chain hood with

Chinese helmet from the eighteenth century *forged of two plates of iron. It is decorated with silver, and it has a chain veil around it.*

a small round plate on top, had been very popular. Round shields were popular throughout the whole Turkish army. They were made of leather, copper, steel, or bronze. Shields woven of willow wicker were called kalkans. Each wicker was carefully wound with silk or cotton thread, the color of which created on the surface of the shield ornamental motifs such as those on Oriental carpets. The center of the shield was strengthened by a metal bulge and was lined with cloth and special pads on the armgrip. Kalkans resisted the cuts of sabers and were also able to catch enemies' arrows.

Equestrian armor deserves special mention. Heavily armored Persian soldiers protected their horses with caparisons, which were covered with

Complete Persian armor of the eighteenth century. *The helmet, like the shield, is decorated with gilded ornamentation. The chain mail consists of chains 10 mm (0.4 in) in diameter. Richly decorated vambraces are included in the armor.*

metal or metal plates and supplemented by
a forehead plate as were worn by the horses of
the Persian heavy cavalry. The officers of the
Turkish Sipahi also covered their horses with
chain caparisons combined with metal plates of
various sizes and shapes.

China has an immensely rich and long history
of protective armor. Bronze helmets dating from
the second millennium B.C. were among the first
discovered by archaeologists. In China the so-
called *soft protective outfit* dominated for
centuries. Its basic material was hard tanned
leather. Two variations of this outfit existed. The
first was called a *kia* and consisted of four-
cornered leather plates quilted onto one

Armor from Iran. *Reinforcing
plates worn over chain armor
are decorated with etched
ornamentation and silver
encrustation.*

Complete samurai armor from the eighteenth century *with the coat of arms of Dakiga-Hiwa on the helmet.*

another. The second type, *kiai*, was made of overlapping leather scales that were rounded at the ends. The original material was rhinoceros leather, but in the times of the Chan dynasty, after the extinction of these animals in the area, armor was made of bull leather. Later, metals such as copper, bronze, and iron were used for both types of armor. Nomads from the Middle East brought chain mail to China, but it did not become very popular. The Chinese cavalry started to use leather mail and helmets and similarly constructed caparisons to protect their horses. Under the rule of the Tang dynasty, the range of armor types expanded notably. Some sources from that time even mention thirteen different kinds of protective armor made either of metal or of cloth and leather. We can trace

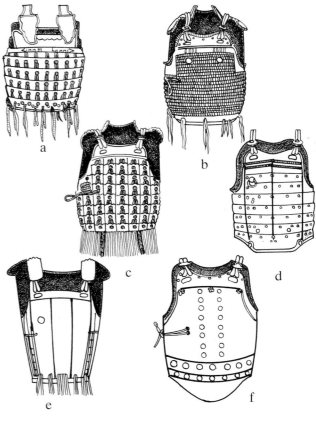

Types of Japanese cuirasses:
a) *Mogami-dó*
b) *Tachi-dó*
c) *Nuinobe-dó*
d) *Yokohagi-dó*
e) *Sendai-dó*
f) *Hotoko-dó*

not only plate, scaly, chain, and combined mail, but also armor of leather, cotton, felt, and even paper. Later, under the Sung and Ming dynasties, this intriguing armor reached such a level of perfection that it was said to be able to ward off bullets. It was made from ten to fifteen layers of paper that were glued together, then cut into pieces and assembled to make a functional and very lightweight mail. Under the Tang dynasty, the various kinds of brigandine gained increasing popularity. The Mongol invasion in the twelfth century brought certain changes. Different materials began to be combined more and more. As for brigandine, it became standard practice to attach plates to the inside of the garment. *Belt armor* also became quite fashionable at the time, but we do not

Samurai armor of the nineteenth century.

Examples of two complete suits of **samurai armor.**

know many details about its appearance and construction. Probably it was an armor made of vertically arranged metal plates reminiscent of the lorica segmentata of Romans.

The most expensive kinds of armor were the luxurious brigandine *ting kia* belonging to the imperial guards and higher military leaders. They were coats of very expensive materials with medium-sized plates of steel, bronze, or leather attached to the inside. Rivets, often gilded, formed an ornamental pattern on the surface of brigandines. It is possible to see some of these suits of armor in Paris, where they were brought by the French army after it seized them in 1861 from Beijing's imperial summer palace.

Japan is also absolutely unique as far as the evolution of armor is concerned. Over the centuries a kind of ingenious samurai armor, *yoroy,* had been developed in Japan. Its pieces were made of relatively small plates of iron, steel, and leather, but sometimes even of bamboo, bound with silk or leather laces. The color of the connecting ties was a distinguishing sign of individual family clans. The warrior's arms were protected by silk sleeves to which small metal plates and chain links were attached at the top. The armor was supplemented by a big helmet, called a *kabuto,* with a wide neck guard. Its skull was varnished or enameled. There was a decoration on the helmet often in the shape of horns, which would have intimidated the enemy. Sometimes the helmet was elongated to a high spike to make the warrior appear taller. The whole suit of samurai armor was light, enabling almost unlimited motion and at the same time effectively protecting against both arrow and sword cuts. Samurai wore this armor up until the second half of the nineteenth century. Japanese foot soldiers used lighter types of helmets and special mail without coverings for their arms, called *horamake* ("abdomen cover"). A whole range of lighter brigandines existed. After the Tokugawa period (Edo, 1603–1867), complete suits of armor for samurai horses appeared. They included caparisons reinforced by plates and supplemented by brow guards for the horse's head, in the shape of a dragon's mask.

Much more could be said about Oriental armor. There were dozens of varieties of construction, and we have not touched on some other important territories (e.g., Korea). It is especially necessary to realize that, unlike in Europe, the Asian military art of modern times was not modernized very quickly, and the great dependence on traditional ways of fighting meant that Asian styles of armor were used, often in only slightly modified form, for centuries up to modern times. Only in the nineteenth century, when most Asian states were ruthlessly confronted with the more developed European military art, did this state of affairs change.

Armored horse. *Persian equestrian armor consisted of a brow plate and a caparison covered by many small metal plates.*

CONCLUSION

The wars that erupted in Europe in the seventeenth century and the beginning of the eighteenth century brought many new trends to military practice. Instead of mercenary troops, most of the developed countries began to form permanent armies that remained active when military operations were over. On the one hand, there were many advantages to this system, but on the other hand, it caused some serious problems. Permanent and large armies were expensive, not only as far as soldiers' pay was concerned, but also in the maintenance of their armor and equipment. When it became necessary to have one army and to make and buy things in bulk, most armor makers lost their jobs. Another serious issue was the change in battle tactics. Military art was changing with the advent of more sophisticated firearms. Gunpowder played an increasingly important

The front plate *of a Prussian cuirass from the eighteenth century.*

role on the battlefield, and the protection provided by armor was becoming obsolete. The infantry was the first to put aside all their pieces of protective armor and go into battle unarmored.

Later, it was realized that the part of the body in constant danger was the head, and therefore some armies returned to the helmet. It proved its worth against mine fragments and grenades, and has remained in various forms in the equipment not only of the infantry, but also other divisions of the army, up to the present day.

The cavalry also changed its equipment. It was divided into light and heavy troops, and this division was closely connected with the function of separate kinds of cavalry in battle. Protection for the head was preserved in some kinds of cavalry, either as a metal or leather helmet or at least as a tricorn hat reinforced with crisscrossed iron bands. Other pieces of armor disappeared, but not the cuirass (made of one or two pieces)

Austrian cuirassier of the early eighteenth century. *At that time, armor only included the cuirass and helmet.*

The front plate *of the cuirass of an officer of the Habsburg monarchy from the first half of the nineteenth century. A brass wedge on the cuirass symbolized the rank of the officer. Its length indicated the level of rank.*

Helmet *for the officers of the chevalier guards of the Russian empress (1910–14).*

Saxon helmet *for the guards cavalry.*

Helmet *of the Bavarian heavy cavalry bodyguards worn in the years 1852 – 1918.*

Helmet *of the Austro-Hungarian officers of dragoon regiments. This model was used until 1914.*

worn by members of the heavy cavalry (i.e., by cuirassiers). This protection, effective especially in one-on-one combat with cold steel, was used in some countries as late as World War I. Elsewhere — for example, in the Habsburg monarchy — the cavalry put cuirasses aside in the middle of the nineteenth century.

Helmets, and sometimes specially designed and shaped mail, were also worn by members of special units who were in contact with explosives and ammunition. Mail was especially effective in protecting against shrapnel.

It cannot be said that armor ever completely disappeared from the battlefield. European soldiers, even in the nineteenth century during the colonial wars, met fighters wearing armor, often of very old forms. Not only was Oriental armor used in battle (in India, China, and elsewhere), but so were the shields of African tribes and Native Americans.

It is necessary to remind ourselves that components of protective armor were not used only by soldiers. For instance, policemen have covered their heads with helmets, some of which

Helmet *as worn by the enlisted ranks of Russian dragoon regiments (1910).*

even have movable visors, although unlike the knightly ones, policemen's visors are of transparent material. Shields have also become an effective part of police equipment. In army and police units, mail as protection for the body has found its modern-day counterpart in the very effective bulletproof vest. It is therefore obvious that protective armor has not yet left the stage of history.

For thousands of years developments in protective armor have kept pace with forms of violence and technical progress. However, we should not forget that the weapons of war are often used with success in civil areas, too. Helmets made of different materials, in shapes designed by technicians so as to be of the greatest use, cover the heads of various professionals — firemen, construction workers, miners, and so on. They are used in various sports; even in some especially dangerous sports like football or ice hockey, the whole body of the player is covered by special protection that is in many ways reminiscent to us of the armor of medieval knights.

Armor of sapper *from World War I. It served as protection against shrapnel.*

British horseman
with a cork helmet.